Teacher's
MANUAL

to

Warriors Don't Cry

By Ann Maouyo

Talent Development Secondary Publications
Center for Social Organization of Schools
Johns Hopkins University
Baltimore

© 2014 by Johns Hopkins Talent Development, All Rights Reserved
These materials were developed by the Talent Development Secondary Program of
The Center for Social Organization of Schools
The Johns Hopkins University, C.S.O.S., 2701 N. Charles Street, Suite 300, Baltimore, Maryland 21218
Permission is granted to copy and distribute reproducible pages only for classroom use. Other reproductions without permission are prohibited.
Cover photo: http://en.wikipedia.org/wiki/File:101st_Airborne_at_Little_Rock_Central_High.jpg

Table of Contents

To the Teacher	i
Planning and Preparation	1
Introduction and Chapters 1 - 4	4
Chapters 5 - 8	21
Chapters 9 - 14	38
Chapters 15 - 18 and Epilogue	52
Selection Review reproducibles	66
Literature Test reproducibles	74
Vocabulary Test reproducibles	82

TALENT DEVELOPMENT SECONDARY (TDS)
ENGLISH LANGUAGE ARTS DIVISION
MISSION STATEMENT

RESPONDING TO THE CHANGING NATURE OF LITERACY BY PROVIDING STUDENTS WITH SKILLS THAT WILL ENDURE BEYOND THE CLASSROOM

Student Team Literature Discussion Guides are designed to support teachers with organizing literacy instruction to respond to the needs of diverse student populations while striving to meet the growing instructional demands of state and district college- and career-readiness standards.

Using whole-class structures, peer discussion, and teacher modeling, this instructional framework affords students regular opportunities to engage in oral language, critical analysis and exploration of information extending to real world applications. Students intuitively deepen understanding of content and develop their inferring and evidence-gathering skills through ongoing exposure to inductive learning, a powerful strategy underlying higher-order thinking and 21st century skills. Teachers routinely facilitate small-group and whole-class discussions to help students apply academic language and develop new insights and perspectives as they read various types of authentic texts. Teachers are also encouraged and equipped to use a variety of informational texts in conjunction with literary works, and to provide students with the skills they need to comprehend these increasingly complex texts. Through reading and writing for different purposes and from multiple perspectives, students move toward the self-regulated learning and independent thinking required to function in today's society.

In the midst of the flow of information surrounding adolescent literacy, we recognize the significant role that motivation plays in the lives of adolescent learners. The instructional design and materials used in the TDS program enable students to exercise mental processes needed to comprehend, communicate, reason, evaluate, and persevere. Students take ownership of learning experiences and make choices within a responsive, student-centered classroom environment.

With the growing demands of the 21st century, the TDS ELA Discussion Guides offer flexibility and guidance to teachers who seek specific focus and clarity when planning instruction. Teachers are able to build instructional modules around core reading selections using existing approaches and activities contained in the Discussion Guides. This approach helps establish historical and factual connections, and addresses specific assessments, standards and skills in the context of teaching the core reading selections. Using this method to planning and teaching literacy, classroom teachers and TDS instructional support staff can effectively collaborate around core approaches to promote achievement for all students in the 21st century.

To the Teacher

This Teacher's Manual is part of a research-based, cooperative approach to teaching literature developed by the Talent Development Secondary Program at the Johns Hopkins University. This approach, called Student Team Literature, strengthens students' thinking, reading, writing, and social skills. In Student Team Literature, students read quality books and work in learning teams using *Student Discussion Guides* that lead them to become critical thinkers, expand their working vocabularies, and broaden their knowledge of the writer's craft. Guides are available to support study of over 70 novels, biographies, and short story and poetry collections. Students read the literature and work through a Student Discussion Guide using a weekly cycle of instruction.

Each Student Discussion Guide includes the following components:

- **Vocabulary Lists** expose students to terms they need to know in order to understand what they are reading.

- **Starred High Frequency Words** are those that students acquire for their working vocabularies, as they occur often in many contexts. Students learn to use these words in meaningful sentences that include context clues to show understanding of the new words.

- **Writer's Craft Boxes** provide information about aspects of the writer's craft (e.g., flashbacks, figurative language) that students encounter in the literature. Craft Boxes can be used as the basis for mini-lessons.

- **Questions** and **Graphic Organizers** lead students to analyze the literature, organize information, and better understand the writer's message.

- **Make a Prediction** and **What If? Boxes** lead students to establish expectations about what will come next in their reading.

- **Selection Review** questions and answers are used by pairs of students to prepare for literature tests.

- **Literature-related Writing** suggestions lead students to respond to literature and try various forms of writing.

- **Extension Activities** give students opportunities to express themselves in response to the text through art, drama, research, and other activities.

- **So, You Want to Read More...** suggests books for independent reading that match the one students have read in theme, genre, or topic.

- **About the Author** provides biographical information, as well as listing some of the writer's other works.

In addition to these sections, each Teacher's Manual also includes:

- a **Summary** of the book or literary work

- a **Building Background** section with suggestions for preparing students to read the literary work

- a **Preview/Predict/Purpose** section with questions that lead students to establish expectations before beginning to read

- **Guided Discussion** questions and suggestions for whole-class discussions

- **Listening Comprehension/Read Aloud Connections** identifying relevant literary elements and devices and listing short works that include these features, which teachers can use to prepare and present *Listening Comprehension* lessons (a teacher read-aloud/think-aloud activity that serves as a companion to Student Team Literature)

These materials can be used within or outside the context of the Student Team Literature program, although we believe teachers who have been trained in the program make the best use of them. (Please see below for teacher training contact information.)

About the Literature

The most effective motivation for adolescent readers lies in the relevance of the literature they are presented. Poor or reluctant readers are particularly in need of relevance in the written word. They need to see themselves in the pages they turn.

Today's adolescents are fortunate; never have they had so much quality literature available that reflects their experiences, their problems, and their cultures. The driving force behind Student Team Literature is making accessible the best of middle grades literature. Discussion Guides have been written for a wide variety of literary works at every readability level, from high interest/low readability selections to classic literature used in middle grades English language arts instruction for over twenty-five years.

Talent Development Secondary Program

The Weekly Instruction Cycle

Discussion Guides enable teachers to lead learning teams through literary works in a cycle of activities that includes **direct instruction**, **team practice and discussion**, and **individual assessment**. After careful preliminary vocabulary instruction, students: (1) read a selected text portion silently; (2) complete (optional) Partner Reading, which gives poor readers and second language learners additional practice to build fluency by reading excerpts aloud; (3) discuss with their partners possible responses to questions and activities in Student Discussion Guides; and, (4) write individual responses to the questions and activities.

Discussion Guides and Cooperative Learning

Discussion Guides are designed to be used in the classroom in the context of cooperative learning. Cooperative learning requires students to learn and exercise many social and academic skills, beginning with the most basic, such as active listening and staying on task. For that reason, introducing students (and teachers, during professional development) to Student Team Literature typically involves direct instruction in relevant skills. The teacher determines the skills to be taught (one at a time), the order in which they will be introduced, and students' readiness to add new skills. Instruction includes discussion of the skill and its importance; completion of a T-chart to show what the skill looks and sounds like (making abstract social skills more concrete for students); and modeling and role-playing use of the skill. As students apply the skills in daily classroom activities, teachers monitor and reinforce their use. Students gradually internalize the skills, creating a cooperative learning climate that has an important positive impact on classroom management and academic achievement.

Assessment

Three assessment tools are available to teachers who use Student Team Literature guides. Each week, after quizzing each other in a process called "Selection Review," students take **literature tests** that require short constructed responses. **Vocabulary tests** assess students' ability to compose meaningful sentences using the high frequency words they have studied in the context of the literature. These Selection Reviews, literature tests, and vocabulary tests are provided on reproducible pages at the end of each Teacher's Manual. In addition, students can practice their standardized test taking skills in relation to the literary work they have studied by taking Standardized Reading Practice Tests that are similar in format to the standardized tests used in school districts throughout the country. Standardized Reading Practice Tests must be ordered separately.

Ordering information

The Talent Development Secondary program offers Teacher's Manuals, Student Discussion Guides, and a Standardized Reading Practice Test booklet including reproducible assessment pages.

- To place an order, call 410-516-4339 or email tds@jhu.edu. The complete Talent Development Secondary materials catalog is available online on our website (see below).

- For teacher training or more on our English language arts, math, science, or social studies programs, contact Maria Waltemeyer at 410-516-2247 or mwaltemeyer@jhu.edu

- Also visit our website at
    www.talentdevelopmentsecondary.com/curriculum

Warriors Don't Cry

By Melba Patillo Beals

TEACHER'S MANUAL
Suggested length of time to be spent on this memoir: 4 weeks

Summary

Warriors Don't Cry is a memoir by Melba Patillo Beals describing her experiences as one of the nine African-American students who participated in the historic integration of Central High School in Little Rock, Arkansas, in 1957 and 1958. Growing up in Little Rock's middle class African-American community, Ms. Beals was painfully aware of the "invisible line" of demands and restrictions created by white society. When Melba was selected to integrate Central High School, her family, although fearful, considered the situation a God-given responsibility. After Arkansas's Governor Faubus ordered the National Guard to keep the African-American students out, President Eisenhower sent the 101st Airborne Division to protect the students as integration was resumed. However, the African-American students lived in constant fear during the ensuing months. Isolated from one another and ostracized by most white classmates, they were ridiculed, threatened, and even physically attacked and abused. When the 101st Airborne was withdrawn, their tormentors grew bolder. By Christmas one student, Minnijean Brown, was suspended for her alleged role in a cafeteria incident. A second incident resulted in expulsion. Segregationists tried to goad the other eight students so that they would also be expelled. Melba found an unexpected ally in Link, a white student who secretly warned her of the segregationists' plans. Despite the constant harassment, the eight students completed their year, and Ernest Green, a senior, graduated with his class. Melba, however, finished high school in California, where she found healing and restoration living with the McCabes, the warmhearted family of a white college professor. The book's epilogue describes the emotional thirty-year reunion of the "Little Rock Nine" on the steps of Central High School.

Teachers should be aware that dialogue in the book includes racial epithets typical of the time period.

About The Author

Melba Patillo Beals grew up in Little Rock, Arkansas. She began writing as a young child when her grandmother bought her a diary and suggested she write down her thoughts and experiences in the form of letters to God. Her contact with journalists during the integration crisis interested her in a career in journalism. After completing high school in California, she attended San Francisco State University. She earned a graduate degree in broadcast journalism and film from Columbia University in New York, worked as a news reporter for NBC for seven years, then began her own public relations firm. She is currently the emeritus chairperson of Communications and Media Studies at the Dominican University of California.

Building Background

Ask students what they know about the civil rights movement in the 1950s. This was the decade during which racial segregation in America was seriously challenged for the first time. Review with students what life was like under segregation. Remind them that in the 1896 case *Plessy vs. Ferguson*, the United States Supreme Court had declared that "separate but equal" treatment of people based on race was legal and constitutional. This allowed state governments to segregate public institutions into facilities that were certainly separate but most definitely not equal. The 1954 Supreme Court decision *Brown vs. Board of Education* finally overturned the "separate but equal" policy and mandated the integration of public education throughout the country. This decision met with resistance in most southern states – resistance not only at a political level, but also in the form of sharp and often violent hostility toward African Americans involved in the integration process. Explain to students that *Warriors Don't Cry* is the account of what integration cost nine courageous teenage students in Little Rock, Arkansas.

Listening Comprehension/Read Aloud Connections

Warriors Don't Cry is a **memoir.** To focus on the broader literary form of autobiography, read chapter one of the *Narrative of the Life of Frederick Douglass, Author: A True Story* by Helen Lester, George Ella Lyon's *A Sign, Yes I Can* by Neil Smith, or selections from *When I Was Your Age,* edited by Amy Ehrlich, or *Just Like Me: Stories and Self-Portraits by Fourteen Artists,* compiled by Harriet Roehmer.

Characterization is essential in this work. To focus on characterization, read Patricia McKissack's *Flossie and the Fox*, Alice Walker's *To Hell With Dying*, Patricia Polacco's *Chicken Sunday* and *My Ol' Man*, or Margaret Hodges' *St. George and the Dragon*.

Beals' account is full of **irony**. Examples of irony can be found in *Imogene's Antlers*, by David Small, *Mufaro's Beautiful Daughters*, by John Steptoe, or *The Sweetest Fig,* by Chris Van Allsburg. The book also makes frequent use of **figures of speech**; for examples of these, read Lyn Littlefield Hoopes' *The Unbeatable Bread*, Jane Yolen's *Owl Moon*, Joyce Carol Thomas' *I Have Heard of a Land*, or Marie Bradby's *More Than Anything Else.*

Want To Read More

If you enjoyed reading *Warriors Don't Cry*, you might also enjoy reading Ellen Levine's *Freedom's Children*, a collection of first-hand testimonies of young people involved in the civil rights movement, or Sheyann Webb's *Selma, Lord, Selma: Girlhood Memories of the Civil-Rights Days*. Or you might prefer Christopher Paul Curtis' *The Watsons Go to Birmingham – 1963*, a Newbery Award-winning novel set around the same period that is both humorous and serious at the same time.

To help students grasp the use of **idioms**, find examples in Peggy Parrish's *Amelia Bedelia* books. **Headlines** and **summarizing** are also important concepts found in Beals' memoir; to focus on these, you might want to turn to your daily or weekly local newspaper.

Preview/Predict/Purpose

Have students **preview** the book by reading the back cover. Also ask them to look at the images and the text on the front cover. Ask them to think about the book's title. Why do they think this account is titled *Warriors Don't Cry*?

Have students **predict** how Melba learned to deal with those who harassed, tormented, and abused her.

Invite students to set a **purpose** for reading. They may want to learn more about the historic struggle for school desegregation and its effects on ordinary people. They might want to learn the secrets that enabled Melba to survive in the face of overwhelming odds. They might want to think about how Melba's experience can help them in their lives today.

Discussion Guide #1

Introduction and Chapters 1 - 4 (pages xi-xii and 1-46)

Write the starred words from the **VOCABULARY LIST** on the next page and their definitions on chart paper or sentence strips that will remain posted throughout the time that students work on the Discussion Guide.

Prepare a **Vocabulary Prediction Chart** (see illustration below) for students to complete after you have introduced the reading selection and the **VOCABULARY LIST**, and before they have begun to read. The chart contains categories into which starred words from the list are to be placed. Students predict how each starred word relates to the reading selection, or if it is impossible to predict its relationship. Categories can be adjusted according to the type of literature being read.

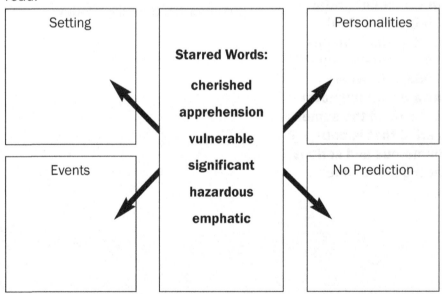

First, read aloud the list of words in the order in which they appear. Second, reread the words and have students repeat each one after you. Third, ask students if they know the definitions of any of the words. Confirm correct definitions, or, in the case of multiple meaning words, identify definitions that match the context in which the words are used in the poems. Next, ask students if they recognize parts of unfamiliar words. If students' decoding skills are below level, stress at this time the sounds of syllables — especially in starred words. In all cases, use this time to focus on identifying the meanings of any prefixes, suffixes or roots that are contained in unfamiliar words, and lead students to formulate definitions based upon the meanings of their parts. Finally, provide definitions for any words that remain undefined. **(Definitions of starred words are in the glossaries that follow the Vocabulary Lists. Definitions are *not* provided for the other words in the Vocabulary Lists.)**

Reread the list in random order and have students repeat each word after you. Then point to the words in random order and have the students pronounce each one without your assistance. Return to any words that students have difficulty pronouncing until they can pronounce them correctly. **This process will be repeated each day that students are working on a particular Discussion Guide, so if students still have difficulty pronouncing some of the words, they will have other opportunities for practice and correction.**

Next, lead students in completing the **Vocabulary Prediction Chart.** The importance of this activity lies in encouraging students to make logical connections between what they have been told about the reading selection and specific vocabulary words. **Being correct about predictions is not important; the thought process required to make predictions is.**

The graphic organizer should be put on chart paper so that the list can remain posted as students read the section of the reading selection in which the words first appear. Introduce words in subsequent Discussion Guides similarly.

Vocabulary List A

heroine (p. xi)	coddle (p. 3)	chastising (adj., p. 9)
integrated (p. xi)	abandoned (p. 3)	resign (p. 10)
compel (p. xi)	confining (adj., p. 3)	*significant (p. 10)
quell (p. xi)	humiliating (adj., p. 3)	anxious (p. 10)
endured (p. xi)	segregation (p. 3)	peering (p. 13)
copious (p. xi)	painstakingly (p. 3)	quivering (adj., p. 13)
ensuing (adj., p. xi)	bout (p. 4)	insistent (p. 13)
elapsed (p. xi)	concessionaire (p. 4)	*hazardous (p. 13)
enabling (p. xi)	*cherished (adj., p. 5)	overpowering (adj., p. 14)
recounted (p. xi)	tattered (adj., p. 5)	lapse (v., p. 14)
recollections (p. xii)	visible (p. 5)	muster (p. 16)
conveys (p. xii)	gourmet (adj., p. 5)	redeem (p. 18)
firestorm (p. xii)	constantly (p. 7)	access (p. 19)
destiny (p. 1)	resisted (p. 7)	opposed (p. 20)
uproar (p. 1)	increasingly (p. 7)	petition (p. 20)
forceps (p. 1)	*apprehension (p. 7)	injunction (p. 20)
massive (p. 2)	*vulnerable (p. 7)	soar (p. 21)
reluctantly (p. 2)	continually (p. 7)	sauntered (p. 21)
inserting (p. 2)	aroma (p. 8)	vibrated (p. 23)
convulsing (p. 2)	festive (p. 8)	*emphatic (p. 23)
irrigate (p. 2)	ominous (p. 9)	inquisition (p. 23)
indignant (p. 2)	cowered (p. 9)	

Special Glossary

irrigate - here, to wash with a healing and cleansing solution

Epsom salts - magnesium sufate salt, dissolved in warm water to treat inflammation, infection, and various other medical conditions

mahogany - a hard, reddish-brown tropical wood used for furniture

soufflé - a main dish made with egg whites, similar to a puffy omelet

hostler - here, a maintenance worker for train engines

Glossary of Starred Words

cherished - precious; treasured

apprehension - fear; worry; anxiety

vulnerable - in danger of being harmed or attacked

significant - important; meaningful

hazardous - risky; dangerous

emphatic - definite; firm; forceful

Sample Meaningful Sentences for Starred Words

1. Mother was beside herself with worry when she couldn't find the **cherished** pearl necklace passed down from her grandmother.

2. Janice had not done her homework, so when Mr. Park announced a pop quiz, she was filled with **apprehension** that she might fail.

3. I feel very **vulnerable** when I walk through that alley alone because of the tough older boys who hang out on the street corner.

4. The news broadcast was filled with unimportant local stories instead of **significant** national or world events.

5. My brother has a **hazardous** construction job walking around on girders hundreds of feet in the air, but the danger doesn't seem to bother him.

6. Mom's order to do our homework first was very **emphatic**, and her firm, insistent tone told us she would not accept any excuses.

The Writer's Craft

Memoir

An *autobiography* is an account of someone's life, written by that person. You can see some of the roots of this word: auto (self) + bio (life) + graphy (writing). Many people have written autobiographical accounts of their lives. A **memoir** is an autobiographical account that focuses on just one portion of a person's life.

continued...

Warriors Don't Cry is a memoir that recounts the role of the writer, Melba Patillo Beals, in the historic integration of Central High School in Little Rock, Arkansas, in 1957. Although most of the book focuses on that eventful and challenging year, the first two chapters briefly tell the story of Melba's early life. As you read, notice how these chapters present Melba's childhood experiences with racism and the ways that her family background prepared her to deal with the challenges she would face at Central High School. How do these chapters help you to better understand the realities of life for African Americans under segregation? What insights do they give you into Melba's personality and point of view?

Situational irony

Situational irony exists when what actually happens is very different from what one would expect. Suppose you were playing baseball and the worst player on the team was the only one who scored a run in a particular game. That would be an ironic situation! As you read these chapters, watch for *ironic situations*, in which reality turns out to be very different from what one might expect.

DISCUSSION QUESTIONS AND ACTIVITIES

Section I. Read the Introduction and Chapters 1 and 2 (pages xi-xii and 1-23). Discuss your responses to the questions and activities with a classmate. Then write your answers separately.

1. **What do we learn from the Introduction about the way this book was written? Why do you think the author felt it was important to include this information at the very beginning of the book?** We learn from the Introduction that the account found in the book is based on the diary entries that Melba kept during the year that she attended Central High School, as well as notes taken and newspaper articles collected by her mother, a high school English teacher. We also learn that the writer was unable to write the book in the first years after the integration experience because the memories were too painful for her, but that she returned to it after time had healed some of those wounds. The writer probably includes this information here be-

cause she anticipates that some readers might think that she is exaggerating or that her memories from such a long time ago may not be accurate. She wants her readers to know that the accounts found in the book are substantially accurate and are based on documents collected as the events took place. She wants to establish the credibility of her story in the reader's mind.

2. **Why did Grandma India believe that God had shown a special interest in Melba's family? What supported her belief that Melba in particular had a special role to play in God's plans?** Grandma India believed that since God had blessed the family with good health and good brains, he expected a special effort from them in discipline, praying, and hard work. She claimed that Melba in particular had a special role to play in God's plans since she had been saved from what seemed like certain death only days after her birth.

3. **List three specific examples of the impact of racism on Melba's life as a young child. How did Melba deal with these painful experiences?** Melba's first experience with racism occurred shortly after her birth. She almost died because nurses at a "white" hospital failed to give her the treatment that the doctor had ordered, claiming that they were not in the practice of "coddling" black people. Another painful experience occurred when Melba, age 5, tried to pay for a ride on the merry-go-round with white children. She was sent away with the angry explanation that there was "no room" for her, despite the obvious empty saddles. Several years later, Melba watched her parents and grandmother cower in humiliation and fear when the white grocer overcharged them and refused to consider their objections. Melba talked with her grandmother and sometimes her mother about the unfairness she observed. Her grandmother bought her a diary that locked in which she could write her thoughts as letters to God.

4. **Explain why Melba decided she would have to keep up with the Supreme Court's decisions in civil rights cases. What was *ironic* about Melba's terrifying experience on May 17, 1954?** Melba decided she would have to keep up with the Supreme Court's decisions because a white man tried to rape her in his

anger over the *Brown vs. Board of Education* ruling on school integration. This frightening experience was ironic because a day of victory for African Americans turned into a day of terror for Melba. Another irony in this experience is the fact that Marissa, an older girl who was considered mentally unstable and whom Melba had always feared, was the one who saved Melba from her attacker by hitting him in the head with a book bag.

5. **Why did Melba sign her name to a list of African-American students who wanted to attend all-white Central High School? Why do you think she did not tell her family that she had signed this list?** Melba signed the list of students wanting to attend Central High School because she had often passed Central High and wondered what it would be like to go to school there. She also hoped that integrating the schools would lead to other doors of opportunity being opened to African Americans, giving them access to equal treatment in movie theaters and other public places. Perhaps she did not discuss it with her parents at first because it seemed so far off; the integration was scheduled to begin two years later. As the time grew nearer, she did not talk to them about it because she assumed that white interest groups would block the integration and it would not take place.

6. **What did Melba find unusual and exciting about her vacation visit to Cincinnati, Ohio? What dreams did her father's phone call cut short?** Melba was fascinated by the freedom from segregation she found in Cincinnati. She was invited to dinner at the home of her aunt and uncle's white neighbors. She went to a drive-in movie with them and their daughter. When she went downtown with her mother and grandmother, they did not have to step aside to let white people pass. They could touch the merchandise in the stores without incurring suspicion, and they were free to eat at the lunch counter. They even went to a restaurant where a white waiter took their orders. Melba was entertaining dreams of staying in Cincinnati to finish high school when her father called to say that she was among the students selected to integrate Central High School.

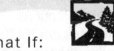

What If:

How do you think Melba's life might have been different if she had *not* signed up to attend Central High School?

> **Guided Discussion:**
> Discuss some of the key questions and activities in Section I. Also, feel free to ask questions not included in the Discussion Guide. As you discuss the questions raised in the Writer's Craft Box on Memoirs, alert students to the fact that the first two chapters help readers understand the impact of segregation on Melba since childhood, as well as the values and the faith in God that her family had instilled in her from a young age. These factors will prove crucial in her response to the difficulties she will have to face.

 ## Vocabulary Prediction Check-up

Return to the vocabulary prediction chart, and use it to check the predictions students made prior to reading this section of the book. Remind students that, even if their predictions did not prove true, the value was in making them.

Vocabulary List B

consumed (p. 24)
petite (p. 24)
sole (adj., p. 25)
dwindling (v., p. 25)
analysis (p. 25)
subtle (p. 25)
regal (p. 26)
pallor (p. 26)
hue (p. 26)
sleek (p. 26)
executed (p. 26)
stature (p. 26)
meticulous (p. 26)
intense (p. 26)
stable (adj., p. 26)
*individualists (p. 27)
feisty (p. 27)
restore (p. 28)
maintain (p. 28)
forcible (p. 29)
contemplation (p. 29)
erect (adj., p. 29)
agony (p. 29)

notified (p. 29)
*federal (p. 30)
vulgar (p. 30)
halt (v., p. 31)
lingered (p. 33)
encircle (p. 33)
maneuvered (p. 34)
craned (p. 34)
destination (p. 34)
clusters (n., p. 35)
span (n., p. 35)
jostling (p. 35)
riveted (adj., p. 35)
muffled (n., p. 35)
frenzy (p. 36)
trance (p. 36)
vile (p. 36)
furor (p. 36)
hub (p. 36)
despite (p. 36)
predicament (p. 37)
triumph (n., p. 37)
*futile (p. 37)

hulking (adj., p. 37)
peril (p. 37)
siege (p. 37)
enlisted (v., p. 38)
accosted (p. 38)
surge (n., p. 39)
ushered (p. 40)
bayonets (p. 41)
mused (p. 41)
ample (p. 41)
pondering (p. 41)
quavered (p. 41)
battered (adj., p. 41)
weary (p. 41)
wrenched (p. 44)
plane (n., p. 44)
sliver (p. 44)
reassure (p. 45)
grimmer (p. 45)
pretense (p. 46)
*anticipation (p. 46)
isolated (adj., p. 46)

Glossary of Starred Words

individualists - people who do things their own way instead of following a crowd

federal - appointed by, or having to do with, national (rather than state) government

futile - useless; pointless; in vain

anticipation - expectation; the act of looking forward to something

Sample Meaningful Sentences for Starred Words

1. This team is made up of strong-minded **individualists** who pursue their own goals without worrying about what other people think of them.

2. The state budget has no money for this project, but we hope to receive **federal** funds from Washington to support it.

3. Matty tried to quiet her aunt's baby, but her efforts were **futile**, and the fussy infant only cried harder.

4. Momma reminded me to **extinguish** the candles before we left the room because letting them burn would create a fire hazard.

5. We looked forward with eager **anticipation** to Joaquin's report on South America, since we expected it to be very interesting.

The Writer's Craft

Characterization

Characterization is the way an author develops characters so that readers can picture and understand them. In *Warriors Don't Cry*, of course, the author is describing real people. However, she still uses characterization to make these personalities come alive for the reader.

continued...

There are several different ways we learn about a character. One is the author's *description* of the character. For example, in the first part of chapter 3, the author briefly describes each of the other eight students who participated in the integration of Central High School. However, we often learn more by directly observing *the person's own words and actions*. We also learn about a person by observing *the way other people relate to him or her*. Each of these things is like a piece of a puzzle. When we put them together, we should be able to get a pretty good idea of the individual's personality.

As you read this section, observe the words and actions of Elizabeth Eckford, Mama, and Grandma. What do we learn about their personalities? Do you think this type of characterization is more or less effective than the brief, straightforward descriptions found in the first few pages of chapter 3? Why?

DISCUSSION QUESTIONS AND ACTIVITIES

Section II. Read chapters 3 and 4 (pages 24-46). Discuss answers to the following questions with a classmate, then write your answers separately.

1. **Describe Melba's life when she returned from Cincinnati. What qualities did the nine students integrating Central High School have in common? In what ways did they differ from one another?** When Melba returned from Cincinnati, her life was filled with meetings: with school administrators and officials, with the leadership of the Arkansas NAACP, and with the other students planning to integrate Central High School. The nine participating in the integration were all serious students. They all came from hardworking, church-going families who had raised them to be respectful and well behaved. They all took pride in themselves and were independent thinkers who planned to attend college. However, the nine students differed from one another in many other ways. Some were talkative, while others were quiet. Some were outgoing, while others were more reserved. Some were athletic, while others were physically frail. Some were musically inclined, others less so.

2. **The writer mentions a number of government and community leaders who played an active role in the integration controversy. In the middle column of the chart below, indicate the official position of each leader. In the last column, write down the role each one played in the integration process. (The first line has been filled in as an example.)** Possible answers are shown.

Name	Official Position or Title	Role in the Integration Process
Mrs. Daisy Bates	President of Arkansas State NAACP	• advised students involved in the integration process • accompanied students on the first day of school
Orval Faubus	Governor of Arkansas	• ordered Arkansas National Guard troops to keep African-American students out of Central High
Virgil Blossoms	Superintendent of Schools	• advised students' parents not to come to school with them on the first day
Ronald Davies	Federal District Court Judge	• gave the order for school integration in Little Rock to be carried out
Rev. Dunbar Ogden, Jr.	President of the Little Rock interracial Ministerial Alliance	• accompanied the students on the first day of school

3. **Why did Melba begin to think that integrating Central High School might not be such a good idea after all? Explain why she decided to go through with it in spite of her fears.** Melba began to think that integrating Central High might not be such a good idea because her family received threatening phone calls so frightening that her grandmother had to sit up at night with a shotgun to protect them from attack. Melba wondered how long this situation could be allowed to continue. However, she believed that integrating Central could be the first step in making Little Rock a place like Cincinnati, where African Americans lived without the restrictions and barriers imposed by segregation. She hoped that as white students came to know their African-American peers, they would lose their prejudices.

4. **Why did Melba drive the car home from Central High School the first morning? Why did Melba's mother tell her she must never tell anyone what had happened to them that morning?** Melba and her mother returned home in the car the first morning because they could not reach the rest of the group of integrating students. They helplessly watched the soldiers and the angry crowd harassing Elizabeth Eckford, until they realized that they too were in danger. As they made their escape, Melba's mother was afraid she would not be able to outrun her pursuers. She tossed the car keys to Melba so that she would be able to leave alone if necessary. When they finally reached the car, the crowd was so close on their heels that Melba just had time to slip into the driver's seat, start the car, and get her mother in the passenger side. Melba's mother told her never to tell anyone what had happened because she did not want the white men who had chased them to know their identity or address. She was afraid the men would attack their home if they associated Melba and her mother with the incident that had occurred.

5. **How did Grandma respond to Melba and her mother's thoughts of going back to Horace Mann, the black high school? Why do you think Grandma was not more sympathetic to Melba's fears?** Grandma was totally opposed to Melba and her mother's thoughts of returning to Horace Mann. She said that if the students integrating Central High School backed down, white segregationists would believe they could do anything they wanted to African Americans – perhaps even enslave them again. She sharply reminded Melba that she had never been a quitter before. Grandma probably was not very sympathetic to Melba's fears because she realized that Melba was going to have to be tough in order to get through this experience. Grandma told Melba she was a "soldier on God's battlefield." She expected Melba to learn to rely on God and ignore her pain and fear.

What If:

What if Melba had decided to give up and go back to Horace Mann High School? What do you think the consequences would have been, not only for Melba, but for the other eight students integrating Central High, and for the cause of civil rights?

> **Guided Discussion:**
>
> Discuss some of the key questions and activities in Section II. In addition, feel free to include in your discussion questions that are not in the Discussion Guide. Be sure to discuss the questions found in the Writer's Craft Box on Characterization. Students should observe Elizabeth Eckford's courage and dignity. They should observe that Mama is a woman torn between her determination to see that justice prevails, and her natural fear for her daughter's safety. Grandma is also a strong, determined woman, whose religious faith gives a firm grounding to everything she does. Students will probably agree that characterization is more effective when the writer shows a person's qualities through his or her actions and words, rather than simply providing a brief description.

 Vocabulary Prediction Check-up

Return to the vocabulary prediction chart, and use it to check the predictions students made prior to reading this section of the book. Remind students that, even if their predictions did not prove true, the value was in making them.

 Selection Review

1. **How did the writer make sure that the account found in *Warriors Don't Cry* would be accurate, even though she wrote it many years later?** The writer based her account on many sources written at the time the events were occurring. For example, she used her own personal diary and the notes that her mother took at that time. Her mother had also collected a number of newspaper articles about the school's integration. Because she relied on these sources, the writer is confident that her story is an accurate one.

2. **List some of the problems Melba faced as a child because of racism. What were two situations in which she narrowly escaped tragedy?** As a child, Melba learned that African Americans had to use the worst fountains and rest rooms. She could not ride the merry-go-round at the park. Her parents were forced to back down, embarrassed, when a white grocer overcharged them. As a baby, Melba almost died because a white nurse did not want to give her the proper care that the doctor had ordered. Later, when she was twelve, she was almost raped by a white man who was angry about the Supreme Court decision on the integration of schools.

3. **What did Melba find amazing about Cincinnati, Ohio? Why did she have to return to Little Rock, and how did her life change at that point?** Melba found Cincinnati amazing because there was no segregation. She and her mother could go shopping downtown without stepping aside to let white people pass. They were invited to dinner at the home of her uncle's white neighbor. They could go to a movie with white people or eat dinner in a restaurant served by white waiters. Melba wanted to stay in Cincinnati to finish high school. However, she had to return to Little Rock because she had been chosen to attend Central High School, an all-white school. When Melba arrived in Little Rock, her life and her family's life were taken up with meetings and preparation for the integration.

4. **Melba decided to participate in the integration even though she was afraid for herself and her family. Why? What qualities did she have in common with the other eight students taking part?** Melba was afraid for herself and her family because they received many threatening phone calls. She decided to participate in the integration anyway because she believed this could be the first step toward ending segregation in Little Rock. She hoped the white students would change their attitudes when they got to know African Americans as classmates. Like the other eight students chosen for the integration, Melba was a serious student. She attended church regularly and was respectful and well mannered. Like the others, she was an independent-minded, proud person who planned to attend college.

5. **Describe Melba's frightening experience the first day she was supposed to attend Central High. How did her grandmother deal with Melba's fears and thoughts of quitting?** The first day Melba was to attend Central High School, she and her mother could not get near the school because of the crowd. They

watched soldiers and crowd members bullying Melba's friend Elizabeth. Then they realized that they were also in danger. They just reached their car in time to escape a mob of angry white men. In spite of this, Melba's grandmother would not let her quit and go back to the black high school. She said that if Melba gave up, the segregationists would believe they were free to treat African Americans unfairly. Grandma told Melba that she was a soldier on God's battlefield. She said that Melba must learn not to cry despite her pain and fear.

> ### Informational Text Connections
> Types of informational text with connections to these chapters include:
>
> Age-appropriate articles on the civil rights movement (e.g., *Kids Discover*, encyclopedia articles, history textbook excerpts, etc.)
> Excerpts from Ellen Levine's *Freedom's Children*
> Archived newspaper or magazine articles on school desegregation
> A short biography of Daisy Bates
>
> Select a text appropriate to your students' reading level and interests. Have them read and analyze the text using applicable criteria from the Common Core Standards. (Remember that different texts will lend themselves to different approaches for comprehension and analysis.)

 ## Literature-Related Writing

1. Melba began keeping a journal when she was just a child. Keep a **journal** of your own experiences, thoughts, fears and dreams each day for at least a week.

2. A memoir is a longer version of a personal narrative. Write a short **personal narrative** telling about an important event or period in your own life.

3. Think of a person you know well – perhaps a close friend or relative. Write a brief **description** of that person's character in two or three sentences. Then, separately, write a **narrative** (story) about an incident involving that person. In your narrative, show the person's character through his or her words and actions.

Extension Activities

1. With other students, act out the scene in the grocery store (chapter 1).
2. Research the historic Supreme Court decision *Brown vs. Board of Education*. Report what you learn to your classmates.
3. Make an imaginary sketch map of Melba's escape route from Central High School, based on the description found in chapter 4. On your map, show the high school, the National Guardsmen, the crowd, Melba's parking space, and the route she took to her house.

Literature Test

1. **Describe the sources the writer used to make sure the story told in *Warriors Don't Cry* would be accurate.** The writer used her own personal diary entries and her mother's notes, as well as newspaper articles her mother had clipped and collected at the time the events occurred, to make sure her story would be accurate.

2. **Describe two painful experiences Melba had as a child because of racism.** Students should list any two of the following: Melba almost died as an infant because a nurse in a "white" hospital refused to give her proper care. She was not allowed to ride the merry-go-round with white children at the park. Her parents had to back down when a white grocer overcharged them. She was attacked and almost raped by a white man who was angry over the Supreme Court decision on school integration.

3. **What did Melba hope to accomplish by participating in the integration of Central High School? Why was this a difficult and courageous decision on her part?** By participating in the integration of Central High School, Melba was hoping to help end segregation in Little Rock, making it more like Cincinnati, Ohio. She hoped that as white students became acquainted with African-American classmates, they would lose some of their prejudices. This was a difficult and courageous decision because Melba's family had received many terrifying threatening phone calls from segregationists.

4. **After Melba's frightening first attempt to go to Central High School, she felt like giving up on integration. How did her grandmother respond to Melba's fear and discouragement? Why?** Melba's grandmother would not allow her to give up and go back to the black high school. She told Melba that if she gave up, white segregationists would believe they were free to treat African Americans unfairly. She told Melba that as a soldier on God's battlefield, she must learn to face trouble without crying or giving in.

Discussion Guide #2

Chapters 5 - 8 (pages 47-106)

Vocabulary List A

suspension (p. 48)
intact (p. 49)
patent (adj., p. 49)
coax (p. 49)
chaperon (p. 50)
rage (n., p. 51)
revert (p. 51)
*aggression (p. 51)
scowling (adj., p. 52)
grotesque (p. 52)
bigotry (p. 52)
groping (p. 52)
condemn (p. 53)
dispatching (p. 53)
*initiated (p. 53)
construct (v., p. 53)
summons (n., p. 53)
respite (p. 54)
compromise (n., p. 54)
*dilemma (p. 54)
resolved (p. 54)
normality (p. 54)
commanding (adj., p. 55)
overlaying (p. 55)
options (p. 55)
prevail (p. 55)
testify (p. 56)
fret (v., p. 56)
throng (p. 56)
eventually (p. 57)
hypnotized (adj., p. 57)
suitable (p. 57)
genuine (p. 58)
ranks (n., p. 58)
*precedent (p. 59)
advocates (n., p. 59)
incendiary (p. 59)
hooligans (p. 59)
rampaged (p. 59)
preyed (p. 59)
overwhelming (v., p. 59)
crucial (p. 61)
collision (p. 61)
brisk (p. 61)
accustomed (p. 62)
undeniably (p. 62)
forge (v., p. 62)
bailiff (p. 63)
heckling (v., p. 63)
precision (p. 63)
intimidating (adj., p. 63)
imposing (adj., p. 64)
gavel (p. 65)
*preliminary (adj., p. 65)
moot (p. 65)
concede (p. 65)
corralled (adj., p. 65)
gauntlet (p. 66)
encountered (p. 66)
plagued (p. 66)
shabby (p. 66)
sufficient (p. 66)
devise (p. 67)
traumatized (p. 67)
thwarted (p. 68)
piercing (adj., p. 68)

Special Glossary

Ike - popular nickname for U.S. President Dwight D. Eisenhower

states'-rights - referring to the belief in the right of state governments to determine their course of action without the federal government intervening

constitutional - here, concerning the interpretation and application of the U. S. Constitution

Glossary of Starred Words

aggression - feelings of anger or violence

initiated - started; begun; set in motion

dilemma - a problem that is very difficult to solve

precedent - an example that sets a pattern for the future

preliminary - introductory; initial; beginning

Sample Meaningful Sentences for Starred Words

1. Some fans' excitement turned to **aggression** as they screamed insults and threw things on the field at the visiting team.
2. The invention of the electric light **initiated** a whole new way of life for people around the world.
3. Track practices and jazz band rehearsal were held at the same time, so Tiara, who belonged to both groups, had a very difficult **dilemma** to solve.
4. Mom did not let my little sister stay up for the show to avoid setting a **precedent** that would make Candice want to stay up late every night.
5. The **preliminary** trials were held the day before the big track meet in order to select the best runners for the final races.

The Writer's Craft

Summarizing and *Headlines*

A **summary** is a short version of something longer that has been written or spoken. To summarize is to write or say a shortened version of something. Summaries do not contain lots of details (specific bits of information).

continued...

> **Headlines** in newspapers are a kind of summary. Headlines are shortened versions of the news stories that follow them. In chapter 4, we read the following two headlines:
>
> FAUBUS CALLS NATIONAL GUARD
> TO KEEP SCHOOL SEGREGATED
>
> and:
>
> JUDGE ORDERS INTEGRATION.
>
> Notice that these headlines contain no details, just a general idea. As you read the next two chapters, you will find more headlines. The author quotes headlines to introduce new stages in the students' struggle to integrate Central High School. Notice how the reporters who originally wrote these headlines managed to summarize important ideas very briefly. Think about how you could do the same thing for events occurring around you.

DISCUSSION QUESTIONS AND ACTIVITIES

Section I. Read chapters 5 and 6 (pages 47-68). Discuss answers to the following questions with a classmate, then write your answers separately.

1. **Why did Melba try to disguise herself with makeup and "grownup" clothes to go to the wrestling matches? Why do you think she was so upset when Grandma decided she had to stay home?** Melba tried to disguise herself to go to the wrestling matches because white people as well as black attended the matches. Melba was afraid that some of them might recognize her as one of the students involved in the integration and try to harm her or Grandma. Melba was probably upset that she had to stay home because she was counting on "accidentally" meeting Vince, a boy she liked, at the auditorium, since she was not yet allowed to date. She was also upset because not being allowed to go to the matches showed her just how much freedom she was losing because of her participation in the integration process.

2. **When Melba saw the picture of Elizabeth Eckford in the newspaper, she felt both sadness and hope. Why?** When Melba saw Elizabeth's picture in the paper, it made her sad because she saw again all the cruel, jeering faces of the people

tormenting her friend, who stood alone in front of Central High. However, the picture also brought hope to Melba, because a white man had paid for the ad in which the picture appeared, calling on all Arkansas citizens to consider what had occurred and feel shame. Melba was encouraged to think that a white man would have the courage and commitment to pay for such an ad.

3. **In the chart below, list some ways that Elizabeth and her fellow students were supported and encouraged by members of the community, both African Americans and others.** Some possible answers are shown.

People Who Helped	How They Supported The Students
African-American churches and religious leaders	They prayed for the students' protection. They provided a network of safety the students could count on.
Teachers and professional people (both African-American and white)	They provided books and tutoring so the students would not fall behind in their studies.
NAACP leaders and lawyers (including Mrs. Bates and Thurgood Marshall)	They helped the students prepare for court hearings, giving them confidence and a positive attitude.

4. **What did Melba find surprising in the behavior of the journalists she observed? What conclusions did she draw?** Melba was surprised that the white journalists called her "Miss" and treated her with respect. She was also surprised that they seemed to be genuinely friendly with other journalists who were African Americans. She realized that their courage and persistence were essential to the success of the integration process. The attitude of the journalists encouraged Melba to believe that working toward integration was the right thing to do. Watching the journalists at work also encouraged Melba to consider a career in journalism for herself.

5. **Explain why the federal court hearing on September 20, 1957, was so important. What was being decided?** The federal court hearing on September 20 was important because it was supposed to determine whether or not the threat of violence gave Governor Faubus a good reason to use national guardsmen to stop the integration plan.

Talent Development Secondary Program

TEACHER'S MANUAL | 25
Chapters 5 - 8

6. **What did Melba find surprising about the federal court hearing? What was the final result?** Melba found several things about the federal court hearing surprising. For one thing, she had been looking forward to seeing Governor Faubus in person, since a court summons had been served to him. She was disappointed to learn that as an elected official he was not required to appear in person. She was also surprised at how small and how very crowded the courtroom was. She was surprised to see that up close, the national guardsmen were not nearly as imposing as they had seemed. Also, like everyone else, Melba was surprised when the governor's attorneys walked out of the courtroom, claiming that the case raised constitutional issues that required a three-judge panel. However, the end result was that Judge Davies ordered the integration to continue.

What If:

How do you think the situation might have been different if the students involved in the integration had not received the support of the community?

What if Judge Davies had not had the courage to maintain his ruling on the integration of Central High School?

Guided Discussion:

Discuss some of the key questions and activities in Section I. In addition, feel free to include in your discussion questions that are not in the Discussion Guide. As you discuss the Writer's Craft Box on Summarizing and Headlines, make sure that students notice the unique syntax found in headlines. For example, verbs are almost always used in the present tense. Articles *(the, a, an)* are frequently omitted, as are the various forms of the verb "to be" *(is, are)*. Lead students in observing these characteristics in the headlines quoted in chapters 5 and 6.

 Vocabulary Prediction Check-up

Return to the vocabulary prediction chart, and use it to check the predictions students made prior to reading this section of the book. Remind students that, even if their predictions did not prove true, the value was in making them.

Talent Development Secondary Program

Vocabulary List B

unrest (p. 69)	momentum (p. 82)	urgency (p. 93)
periodically (p. 70)	envelop (p. 83)	eerie (p. 93)
hovered (p. 70)	accelerated (p. 83)	caravan (p. 94)
clamor (n., p. 72)	hurling (p. 83)	distraught (p. 94)
winding (adj., p. 72)	subsided (p. 83)	convoy (n., p. 94)
cavernous (p. 72)	registrar (p. 84)	intervals (p. 94)
numb (adj., p. 74)	disheveled (p. 85)	etched (p. 95)
fantasized (p. 74)	mulling (p. 86)	threshold (p. 96)
*treacherous (p. 74)	spewing (p. 86)	placid (p. 97)
ridicule (n., p. 74)	articulate (adj., p. 86)	taunting (n., p. 98)
disoriented (adj., p. 75)	accentuate (p. 87)	browbeat (p. 98)
*compassion (p. 76)	sensations (p. 87)	tarpaulins (p. 100)
obscenities (p. 77)	spacious (p. 87)	pristine (p. 101)
brigade (p. 77)	conducive (p. 87)	exceeded (p. 101)
maze (p. 77)	*contempt (p. 87)	*confronted (p. 101)
menacing (p. 77)	aspirations (p. 88)	steeled (adj., p. 101)
composure (p. 78)	*jeopardize (p. 89)	dispersed (p. 101)
hanky-panky (p. 78)	vigilance (p. 89)	outrageous (p. 102)
reprimand (n., p. 78)	resuming (p. 89)	meekly (p. 102)
transfixed (p. 78)	obstruction (p. 89)	bombardment (p. 104)
ebbing (p. 79)	inset (p. 92)	amended (p. 105)
adjoining (adj., p. 79)	fascinated (p. 92)	demise (p. 105)
anteroom (p. 79)	glistening (p. 93)	persistence (p. 105)
secure (v., p. 82)	briefing (n., p. 93)	

Special Glossary

shorthand - a system of speed writing using symbols, widely used to take down a person's exact words, especially in the time before computers were in use

Glossary of Starred Words

treacherous - dangerous; unsafe; risky

compassion - sympathy; kindness; concern

contempt - scorn; looking down on someone hatefully

jeopardize - to endanger; to put at risk

confronted - challenged; met head on

Sample Meaningful Sentences for Starred Words

1. Lindsey was afraid to climb down the steep mountain slope since the loose, jagged rocks looked slippery and **treacherous**.

2. Mrs. Robinson's **compassion** for the homeless people in the park led her to take them old blankets to use on cold winter nights.

3. "Look, no one challenges *me*, shrimp," Damon told Louie, his mocking voice dripping with **contempt**. "I'm king of the court– just don't forget it."

4. Lawrence worked hard on his history project since he knew a bad grade would **jeopardize** his chance of getting an 'A' in the course and making the honor roll.

5. When we went to the hospital to see Grandma, a security guard in the hall **confronted** us, asking to see our visitor's passes.

The Writer's Craft

Figures of Speech

Figures of speech are expressions in which objects, actions, or situations are described by comparing them with something else. There are many different types of figures of speech. In **similes**, two objects, people, or situations are compared using words such as "like" or "as." For example, chapters 5 and 6 include the following similes:

"...[T]he twisted, scowling white faces with open mouths jeering... clustered about my friend's head *like bouquets of grotesque flowers*." (page 52)

"...[Thurgood Marshall] had a self-assured air about him *as though he had seen the promised land* and knew for certain we could get there." (page 55)

"Thoughts buzzed inside my head *like bees disturbed in their hive*." (page 57)

"Some days it was *as though someone had put me in Grandma's cake mixer*, but I was struggling to be still, not to spin or shudder or shake." (page 59)

continued...

"*Like sardines* we wiggled and pushed, trying to forge a pathway." (page 62)

"The deep voice sounded *like a circus ringmaster* announcing the next act." (page 64)

"Reporters ran for the door *like corralled horses through an open gate.*" (page 65)

Metaphors are another figure of speech. In a metaphor, two unlike things are compared *without* using the words "like" or "as." The writer either states or implies (suggests) that one thing *is* another. Here are two examples of metaphor from chapters 5 and 6:

"[Grandma] was dressed in... a blue suit with a matching hat *that swooped down from its mischievous perch* on the side of her head." (page 49; the hat is described as if it were a bird.)

"...Grandma had said: *'Church is the life's blood* of our community.'" (page 53)

"... Reverend Young... would set off a rescue and construct a *web of safety.*" (page 53)

"I felt a new *fountain of hope* rise up inside me." (page 58)

Personification is a third common type of figure of speech. Personification occurs when an inanimate object or idea is described in terms that would normally be used to describe a person. Here are two examples of personification from chapters 5 and 6:

"As I picked up the newspaper, *headlines leaped out* at me." (page 47)

"That elevator was so full that I could hear *its guts grinding as it struggled* to deliver us to the fourth-floor courtroom." (p. 62)

As you read the next two chapters, see how many more figures of speech you can find. Each time you find a figure of speech, try to determine what is similar about the two things being compared.

TEACHER'S MANUAL
Chapters 5 - 8

DISCUSSION QUESTIONS AND ACTIVITIES

Section II. Read chapters 7 and 8 (pages 69-106). Discuss answers to the following questions with a classmate, then write your answers separately.

1. **In chapter 6, the writer compares Central High School to two types of buildings. What are they? What similarities did she see? What was the *ironic* difference between Central High's appearance and the reality of Melba's life once she got inside?** The writer compares Central High, with its marble floors, stone walls, and long winding hallways, to a museum, or a "huge, beautiful castle" because of its size and its spiral staircases. In Melba's dreams about attending Central, she saw the "huge, beautiful castle" as a wonderful, magical place. She soon found out that it was, instead, a place of danger, full of enemies, whose very size made it that much easier to get lost in – more like the castle of a wicked witch than of a benevolent king.

2. **On one side of the T-chart one below, list some of the unpleasant and frightening things that happened to Melba on her first day at Central. On the other side, list the people who helped her or tried to be kind to her, and describe what they did.** Some possible answers are shown.

Frightening and Unpleasant Experiences	Kind or Helpful People
White students taunted the new black students, calling them names.	Mrs. Huckaby tried to orient the new students.
None of the nine black students were together in homerooms or classes.	Melba's gym teacher treated her pleasantly and warned her when the women came over the fence to attack her.
A woman spat in Melba's face and insulted her.	Mrs. Pickwick, the shorthand teacher, welcomed Melba warmly, and refused to allow other students to be rude to her.
Melba's first period teacher allowed students to heckle her freely in class.	
Classmates threw a volleyball at Melba's head during gym.	Gene Smith, Assistant Chief of Police, insisted on getting all nine new students out of the school safely.
A group of women came over the wall to attack Melba on the playing field, and one of her classmates tripped her as she ran away.	Melba's "guide," although brusque, tried to protect her from harm.
Melba got lost in the halls as she fled from her attackers.	The drivers designated by the police managed to get the students home safely despite the attacking crowds.
Melba heard the policemen discussing whether to let the crowd hang one of the new students in order to get the others out safely.	

Talent Development Secondary Program

3. **Did Melba tell the truth in the article she composed for the Associated Press about her first day at Central High? Explain. Why did she tell the story this way? What would you have done if you were in her place?** Melba's story for the Associated Press was mostly true. However, she downplayed the violence she experienced and overstated the kindness she encountered. Melba did this because she realized that if she told the whole truth, proponents of segregation would seize the opportunity to put an end to integration, claiming that it was too dangerous. Perhaps, too, there was an element of wishful thinking in her account; she seems to describe expressions of kindness and encouragement that she would have liked to receive from fellow students. Answers will vary as to what students would have done in Melba's place.

4. **Why did President Eisenhower send the 101st Airborne Division to Little Rock? How did the soldiers' presence make Melba feel?** President Eisenhower sent in the 101st Airborne Division to protect the African-American students during the integration of Central High. This was necessary because Governor Faubus had effectively refused to use Arkansas state troopers to enforce the federal court's ruling that the integration was to go forward. The soldiers' presence made Melba feel somewhat safer. She was proud that the United States would deploy such a show of military force to ensure that the law was upheld, but also sad that they were obliged to go to such great lengths to do so.

5. **How did the federal troops, particularly her bodyguard Danny, help Melba get through her second day at Central? List the places where Danny was not allowed to go with Melba.** The federal troops took the nine new students to Central in a convoy. Then they formed a square around them until they were safely inside the school. During the day, Danny accompanied Melba in the halls, and even when they were accosted by a crowd of boys, other soldiers appeared to protect her. Danny also gave Melba good advice about staying calm. However, Danny was not allowed to accompany Melba into her classrooms, the cafeteria, the study hall, or, of course, the girls' restrooms and locker room.

What If.

What do you think would have happened if President Eisenhower had not sent the 101st Airborne Division into Arkansas to oversee the integration of Central High School?

Guided Discussion:

Discuss some of the key questions and activities in Section II. In addition, feel free to include in your discussion questions that are not in the Discussion Guide. For example, you might want to ask, *What encouraging signs did Melba see in some of the white students during her second day at Central?* Melba was encouraged to see that a few white girls did smile at the newcomers, and even sat down with them in the cafeteria.

You may have to make sure that students understand the difference between:

- the National Guard, a military unit under the authority of the individual states, in this case Governor Faubus, who initially kept the African-American students out of Central High School; and

- the Little Rock local police department, which for the most part attempted to protect the students and ensure their safety; and

- the 101st Airborne Division, a division of the U.S. Army, under the authority of the President of the United States. The task of the 101st Airborne was to see that the court-ordered integration was executed in a peaceable manner.

Be sure to discuss the questions raised in the Writer's Craft Box on "Figures of Speech." Some of the figures of speech found in Chapters 7 and 8 are as follows. (It is not necessary to discuss every single example with students. Please make sure you have discussed a representative selection, preferably mostly those suggested by the students.)

"Other parents milled about, *looking as if we were being carted off to be hanged.*" (simile, p. 70; point of similarity: a look of doom and despair)

continued...

"It was *like entering a darkened movie theater* – amid the rush of a crowd eager to get seated before the picture begins." (simile, p. 71; point of similarity: hurry and jostling)

"...a row of white people, mostly women, stood staring at us *as though we were the world's eighth wonder.*" (simile, p. 72; point of similarity: a look of astonishment)

"I turned to see the hallway *swallow up my friends.*" (personification, p. 73; point of similarity: they disappeared down its great length)

"I had fantasized about how wonderful it would be to get inside *the huge beautiful castle* I knew as Central High School." (metaphor, p. 74; point of similarity: a huge, awe-inspiring, previously forbidden and therefore magical-seeming building)

"I was disoriented, *as though my world were blurred and leaning to the left, like a photograph snapped from a twisted angle and out of focus.*" (simile, p. 75; point of similarity: sensation of confusion and disorientation.)

"My heart was *weeping...*" (personification, p. 75; point of similarity: feeling of sorrow)

"...the *twisted maze* of the hallway seemed even more menacing." (metaphor, p. 77; point of similarity: a confusing number of paths to choose from)

"...I raced through *a honeycomb* of locker rooms and dead-end hallways." (metaphor, p. 77; point of similarity: many small chambers, seemingly all alike)

"The *ocean of people* stretched farther than I could see – *waves of people ebbing and flowing...*" (metaphor, p. 79; point of similarity: a vast and seemingly endless expanse shifting back and forth)

" '...it seemed *as if I were lost on an island,* an island of strange people, having no way to communicate with them.' " (simile, pp. 87-88; point of similarity: sense of isolation and inability to make meaningful contact with other people)

"There was an eerie hush over the crowd, *not unlike the way I'd seen folks behave outside the home of the deceased* just before a funeral." (simile, p. 93; point of similarity: silence, and a sense of solemnity and respect for the occasion)

continued...

"...the soldiers did not make eye contact as they surrounded us *in a protective cocoon*." (metaphor, p. 95; point of similarity: they were completely surrounded or enveloped) [**Teachers, please note**: The word "as" in this sentence is a preposition of time that means "while" and is *not* used for comparison. For this reason, this sentence contains a metaphor and *not* a simile. You may wish to point this out to students as a reminder that the mere presence of the word "as" is not always a sure-fire indication that a sentence contains a simile!]

"[Being in Mrs. Pickwick's class] was *like being on a peaceful island*." (simile, p. 98; point of similarity: sense of peace and safety from attack)

"[The military camp] *was an absolute beehive* of activity." (metaphor, p. 100; point of similarity: constant, purposeful, highly organized activity)

"Entering the door was *like walking into a zoo* with the animals outside their cages." (simile, p. 102; point of similarity: extreme danger and savage, unpredictable behavior)

"...students were milling about *as though they were having a wild party*." (simile, p. 102; point of similarity: wild, unchecked behavior)

"...students gathered on the school lawn, staring at us *as though they were watching a parade* they hadn't known was coming their way." (simile, p. 103; point of similarity: surprise and a sense of unpreparedness)

"...[We] turned to face the *bombardment of questions* as we made our way to Mrs. Bates' front door." (metaphor, p. 104; point of similarity: being pounded from all sides)

"As we rode home I looked forward to shedding my day *like soiled clothing*." (simile, p. 105; point of similarity: eagerness to set something aside and turn to other things)

 ## Vocabulary Prediction Check-up

Return to the vocabulary prediction chart, and use it to check the predictions students made prior to reading this section of the book. Remind students that, even if their predictions did not prove true, the value was in making them.

Selection Review

1. **Describe some ways that African Americans, and a few white people, showed support for Melba and the other eight students.** Community members showed support in many ways. African-American churches encouraged the students and prayed for them. NAACP leaders and lawyers advised them about the legal hearings. Teachers of both races lent them books and tutored them so they would not fall behind in their schoolwork. A white man paid for an ad in the paper. This ad said all citizens of Arkansas should be ashamed of the hatred and bigotry that had been shown to the students.

2. **In what ways did the journalists' behavior encourage and inspire Melba?** Melba was surprised that the white journalists called her "Miss" and treated her respectfully. She saw that black and white reporters treated each other as friends. She saw that the integration would not be taking place if the reporters had not been so brave and determined to tell the world what was happening. Melba felt even more convinced that integration was right. She thought she might like to be a journalist herself one day.

3. **List some reasons for Melba's feelings of surprise at the federal court hearing. What was decided in the hearing?** Melba was surprised that the courtroom was so small. Also, up close the national guardsmen seemed so ordinary. Melba was very surprised that Governor Faubus did not attend the hearing. Even the governor's lawyers walked out almost as soon as the hearing began. Judge Davies decided that the integration would continue. He said that Governor Faubus had no right to stop it.

4. **What did the Central High School building make Melba think of? Why? Why was this ironic?** Central High School reminded Melba of a museum or a beautiful castle. It was very big and had beautiful stone walls, marble floors, and spiral staircases. This was ironic because Melba soon discovered that Central High School would instead be a place of danger and fear for her.

5. **List some of the good and bad things that happened to Melba on her first day at Central High School. How did she describe her day in her article for the Associated Press?** Melba's first day at Central High School was like a nightmare. People called her names. A woman spit in her face. Students tormented her in class. A group of women even came over the fence to attack

her on the playing field. She lost her way. Worst of all, she heard policemen saying they might let the crowd hang one of the students in order to save the others. However, a few people showed kindness to the students. Mrs. Huckaby, the girls' vice principal, tried to treat them fairly. Melba's gym teacher and her shorthand teacher, Mrs. Pickwick, showed concern for her. The Assistant Police Chief and the police drivers risked their lives to make sure all the students arrived home safely. In her article, however, Melba told only part of the truth. She was afraid that if she told how terrible it really was, the integration would be stopped.

6. **Explain why President Eisenhower sent the Airborne Division soldiers to Central High School. What difference did the soldiers make on Melba's second day of school?** The soldiers were sent to Central High School to protect the nine students and keep the peace. They guarded the students and took them to school. Then a soldier walked through the halls with each student during the day. Melba felt safer on her second day because of the soldiers, especially her "bodyguard," Danny. Still, there were many places where Danny was not allowed to go with her. These places included the classrooms, cafeteria, study hall, and of course the girls' rest rooms and locker room.

Informational Text Connections

Types of informational text with connections to these chapters include:

   Biographical material about Thurgood Marshall or President Dwight Eisenhower

   Local newspaper articles on current events (focus on use of headlines)

Select a text appropriate to your students' reading level and interests. Have them read and analyze the text using applicable criteria from the Common Core Standards. (Remember that different texts will lend themselves to different approaches for comprehension and analysis.)

Literature-Related Writing

1. Choose an incident that occurred during Melba's first or second day at Central High School (for example, the attack on the playing field, the return home in the police cars, or the students' arrival with a military escort on the second day.) Write a **news article** about the incident, as if you were a reporter for a national magazine or newspaper. Then, summarize your article with a brief, snappy **headline**.

2. Write a **personal narrative** describing a frightening or exciting experience in your own life. Try to use **figures of speech** in your narrative to make your description more interesting.

3. Pretend you are one of the soldiers of the 101st Airborne Division. What does the integration of Central High School look like from your point of view? Write a **letter** home to your family telling about your responsibilities and your observations.

 Extension Activities

1. Melba realized that the courage and persistence of the journalists helped lead the nation to take the issue of school integration seriously. Think of an important issue or concern in your own school or community. Do some investigative reporting about this issue. Write an article and/or make a video presentation of your findings.

2. Make an imaginary map of Central High School, based on the description found in the book. Label the office, cafeteria, playing field, locker room, and other places mentioned in the writer's account.

3. Interview someone you know who is a police officer or a member of the armed forces. Ask him or her about crowd control, why it is sometimes necessary, and what strategies are used. Share what you learn with your classmates.

Literature Test

1. **List three things that encouraged Melba as she waited for the court hearing to allow her to go back to Central High School.** Students should mention any three of the following: Melba was encouraged when a white man paid for an ad in the newspaper calling citizens of Arkansas to be ashamed of the bigotry shown to the students. The prayers and support of African-American churches encouraged her. Lawyers and NAACP leaders like Thurgood Marshall and Mrs. Daisy Bates encouraged her. Tutoring and academic help from community teachers encouraged her. The respect, courage, and unprejudiced behavior of the journalists encouraged her.

2. **Describe the outcome of the federal court hearing. Tell why it was important.** In the federal court hearing, Judge Davies decided that the integration was to continue. It was important because he said that Governor Faubus did not have the right to go against the court order and stop the integration. The students were to be allowed to return to Central High School.

3. **How had Melba imagined Central High School in her dreams? What was it really like for her?** When Melba dreamed of entering Central High School, she thought of it as a great beautiful castle. However, her dreams turned into nightmares when she finally went there: students as well as some adults called her names, tormented her, spit at her, and even physically attacked her. The long, spacious hallways and spiral staircases made it easy for her to lose her way.

4. **Why did the 101st Airborne Division come to Little Rock? How did Melba's experience at school change after the soldiers arrived?** The Airborne Division came to Little Rock to protect the students and ensure that the integration was carried out in a peaceful way. After the soldiers' arrival, Melba did not feel quite as frightened. The soldiers escorted the students into school. A "bodyguard" also accompanied each student in the halls during the day. However, the soldiers were not allowed to go into classrooms as well as many other places, so the experience was still frightening and difficult.

Discussion Guide #3

Chapters 9 - 14 (pages 107-173)

Vocabulary List A

engaged (adj., p. 107)
scampered (p. 107)
sarcastic (p.109)
stance (p. 109)
moping (p. 109)
hoopla (p. 110)
archrival (p. 110)
breakneck (p. 111)
pep rally (p. 111)
preoccupied (p. 111)
raspy (p. 112)
notion (p. 114)
disseminating (p. 115)
incommunicado (p. 115)
queasy (p.115)
dither (n., p. 116)
minimum (n., p. 117)
fend (p. 118)
pelting (p. 118)
passive (p. 119)
singed (p. 119)

implored (p. 120)
scuffle (p. 120)
fiasco (p. 120)
reverberated (p. 121)
belligerent (p. 121)
throbbing (adj., p. 121)
searing (adj., p. 121)
pried (p. 122)
dousing (p. 122)
soothing (adj., p. 123)
insure (p. 124)
staunch (adj., p. 125)
brutal (p. 127)
*deteriorated (p. 127)
brooding (v., p. 128)
assess (p. 128)
*mobile (adj., p. 128)
lulled (p. 128)
biding (p. 128)
rhetoric (p. 129)
*obsessed (adj., p. 130)

*exclude (p. 130)
enraptured (v., p. 130)
fatalistic (p. 131)
regained (p. 131)
polarized (adj., p. 132)
*adamant (p. 132)
heathens (p. 132)
stingy (p. 132)
prosecute (p. 134)
agitators (p. 134)
wringing (p. 134)
*console (v., p. 134)
podium (p. 135)
relish (v., p. 135)
garbled (v., p. 135)
contorted (v., p. 135)
intently (p. 135)
trounced (p. 136)
cringed (p. 136)
frivolity (p. 138)

Special Glossary

alkaline - containing a chemical with burning qualities, such as lye

optometrist - a professional who cares for eyes and prescribes glasses, contact lenses, etc.

castor oil - a plant oil often prescribed as a health supplement

gabardine - a heavy cloth with a twill texture used for suits

Glossary of Starred Words

deteriorated - became worse

mobile - able to move about

obsessed - overly focused; thinking of something all the time

exclude - to keep someone or something out

adamant - completely determined; very stubborn

console - to comfort; to cheer someone up

Sample Meaningful Sentences for Starred Words

1. Mama hoped James's report card would improve, so she was very upset to find that his grades had actually **deteriorated** instead.

2. After the surgery, Grandpa couldn't wait to get out of bed and into a wheelchair, so he would be **mobile** enough to get around the house.

3. Jacquie was so **obsessed** with looking good that she spent hours in the bathroom fixing her makeup and trying out new hairstyles.

4. Mom told the boys that it was not fair to **exclude** Teyonna from the game and make her play by herself just because she was a girl.

5. I have to finish my science fair project on time, because Mr. Hanna was very **adamant** that absolutely no late entries would be accepted for any reason.

6. Melissa was so upset after she lost her big race that nothing we could say would **console** her.

The Writer's Craft

Idioms

Idioms are expressions in which words are used to mean something different from their usual or literal meaning. We use idioms every day without even thinking about it – for example, we might say, "I'm flat broke" or "That's right up my alley." But idioms change from one culture to another as well as with the passage of time. For example, some of the idioms you use with your classmates may not be familiar to people of your grandparents' generation or to people from a different part of the country.

A number of idioms are used in these chapters of *Warriors Don't Cry*. Some of them may be familiar to you, while others might not. Here are some examples, along with their meanings:

"He's really **fired up** the segregationists." (p. 115)	– *He's made them angry.*
I was **on edge** (p. 121)	– *I was tense or nervous.*
making **mountains out of molehills** (p. 122)	– *making a big fuss about a minor problem*
the **same song and dance** (p. 129)	– *the same useless speech*
clamming up (p. 131)	– *becoming quiet and withdrawn*
taking its toll of her (p. 131)	– *wearing her out*
she often **took a lot of heat** (p. 131)	– *took a lot of abuse*
ante up (p. 133)	– *to pay or give one's share*
the **King's English** (p. 136)	– *standard English*
...she would **skunk us** again (p. 136)	– *defeat us badly*
"Just **mind your p's and q's**." (p. 138)	– *be very careful*

DISCUSSION QUESTIONS AND ACTIVITIES

Section I. Read chapters 9-11 (pages 107-140). Discuss answers to the following questions with a classmate, then write your answers separately.

1. **In the first column of the chart below, list different ways that Melba was physically attacked at Central High School. In the second column, describe her "bodyguard" Danny's reaction to each attack. In the last column, explain why he reacted (or failed to react) in each situation.** Possible answers are shown (see next page).

Description of Attack	Danny's Response	Reason for This Response
Boys bump into her and kick her in the shins and stomach (p. 108).	Danny just stands over her and motions the boys to move away.	Danny is not allowed to physically fight or argue with the students.
A flaming stick of dynamite is thrown at Melba in the stairwell.	Danny dashes past Melba to put out the flame and give the dynamite to another soldier.	Danny knows the dynamite could kill Melba. His job is to keep her alive.
Some boys try to choke Melba in the auditorium after a pep rally	Danny cannot help Melba.	Danny is not allowed in the auditorium and does not see the boys attack her.
Girls trap Melba in the lavatory stall and throw flaming wads of paper down on her.	Danny cannot help Melba.	The incident occurs on the day that Danny and other soldiers of the 101st are taken out of the school.
A boy throws a burning chemical into Melba's eyes.	Danny moves her quickly to a faucet or water fountain and bathes her eyes over and over.	This attack is serious; the chemical could destroy Melba's eyesight.

2. **How did the administrators at Central High School respond when Melba complained about students attacking her? How did Melba's way of dealing with danger change as time went on?** When Melba complained about student attacks, she was told that the school administrators could do nothing unless a teacher or other adult—not including the soldiers—witnessed the attack and could identify the attackers. Melba gradually realized that she had to learn to take care of herself. Danny's example and advice taught her to stay alert and look confident, no matter how she felt. She learned to ignore small annoyances and insults and to be on her guard to avoid genuinely dangerous threats. She learned to fight back when necessary, and to move on when a problem had been dealt with. She developed the mentality of a soldier on the battlefield.

3. **How did Melba try to recover her "normal" life during the weekend? Did she succeed? Why or why not?** Melba tried to recover her "normal" life by not paying any attention to the news or reading, writing, or talking about the integration. She was

partially successful because her family agreed not to talk about it either, and her mind was kept busy thinking of her date with Vince after church on Sunday. However, at dinner on Sunday Grandma mentioned that the soldiers might be taken out of the school the following week. For the rest of the evening and night Melba worried about what would happen.

4. **The first column of the chart below lists several attempts that were made to solve the problems at Central High School. None of them was very successful. In the second column, explain what went wrong with each "solution."** Possible answers are shown.

Proposed Solutions	Why These Solutions Were Not Successful
The Arkansas National Guard would keep peace and the 101st Airborne would be taken away after its first week in the school.	The Arkansas National Guardsmen just stood around like spectators, making no attempt to protect the students from abuse.
African-American students and segregationist student leaders would come to an understanding if they had a frank discussion in a safe place.	The segregationist students completely misinterpreted the discussion. They later claimed that black students did not want to integrate the school but were being paid to do so by the NAACP.
African-American students and their parents would meet with school officials to discuss ways to resolve tensions and stop abuse of the students.	School officials refused to assume responsibility for the students' safety. They just kept repeating that black students were to avoid responding to their attackers.

5. **Why did Minnijean want so badly to sing in the school Christmas program? Why do you think school officials invited Melba to speak during chapel, but refused to allow Minnijean to sing in the concert?** Minnijean wanted to sing in the program because she believed that white students would accept her if they only heard how well she sang. School officials probably invited Melba to speak during chapel because it was a fairly small, intimate setting, and the students who chose to attend chapel were less likely to be openly hostile. However, the Christmas program was a very large, public event, attended by parents and community members as well as students. Allowing Minnijean to participate would be a very public way of including her as a member of the student body, and the school officials did not care to take that risk.

TEACHER'S MANUAL | 43
Chapters 9 - 14

What If:

One boy thought that Governor Faubus had created a lot of bad feeling when he sent the National Guard to stop integration. Do you agree? How do you think the situation might have been different if he had not sent them?

What do you think might have happened if school officials had given integration their wholehearted support from the beginning?

Guided Discussion:

Discuss some of the key questions and activities in Section I. In addition, feel free to include in your discussion questions that are not in the Discussion Guide. You might want to ask, *What bad news did Melba get during Thanksgiving break? How did she feel?* During Thanksgiving break, Melba learned that the last of the 101st Airborne Division had been withdrawn from Central High. Melba was very sad to think she might never see Danny again.

 Vocabulary Prediction Check-up

Return to the vocabulary prediction chart, and use it to check the predictions students made prior to reading this section of the book. Remind students that, even if their predictions did not prove true, the value was in making them.

Talent Development SecondaryProgram

Vocabulary List B

morsels (p. 142)	jubilant (p. 150)	hoax (p. 159)
profiles (p. 142)	jovial (p. 150)	*turmoil (p. 159)
barrage (p. 142)	eject (p. 151)	ruckus (p. 162)
injurious (p. 142)	embroiled (p. 151)	retaliation (p. 162)
insidious (p. 143)	gingerly (adv., p. 152)	*contends (p. 163)
entrapment (p. 143)	crudely (p. 152)	devastating (adj., p. 166)
afterthought (p. 144)	sorority (p. 152)	
unaware (p. 146)	coveted (v., p. 153)	renowned (p. 166)
fatigue (p. 147)	electrifying (adj., p. 157)	angora (adj., p. 167)
blissful (p. 147)	*incite (p. 158)	eliminated (p. 168)
*intervening (v., p. 149)	proviso (p. 158)	indignities (p. 168)
melee (p. 149)	systematic (p. 159)	immersed (adj., p. 171)

Special Glossary

lost in the shuffle - (*idiom*) forgotten because of so many other things going on

stuck your necks out - (*idiom*) took the risk of standing out individually

Mutt and Jeff - (*idiom*) characters in an early cartoon strip; used to describe any two men often seen together, one tall and the other short

stopped dead in her tracks - (*idiom*) stopped very suddenly

Sputnik - a satellite that the Soviet Union sent into space in 1957 to orbit the earth

Gandhi - (Mohandas, 1869-1948; *also called* Mahatma Gandhi) a Hindu nationalist leader who led the struggle for India's independence from Great Britain, while teaching and practicing non-violent resistance to injustice

Glossary of Starred Words

intervening - interfering; getting involved

incite - to provoke or push someone to do something

turmoil - confusion; trouble; disorder

contends - declares; claims; insists

Sample Meaningful Sentences for Starred Words

1. I am going to let you solve this problem without my help, because I've noticed that by **intervening** I sometimes make things worse for you.

2. The children tried to **incite** the dog to bark by throwing sticks at it and making growling noises.

3. The mayor's remarks threw the meeting into **turmoil** as council members screamed insults and observers jumped up on chairs.

4. When I heard we were having a unit test in science, I was filled with **apprehension**, because I had not studied at all.

5. Marlyse **contends** that it was her brother who started the fight, but he insists it was all her fault.

DISCUSSION QUESTIONS AND ACTIVITIES

Section II. Read chapters 12-14 (pages 141-173). Discuss answers to the following questions with a classmate, then write your answers separately.

1. **Why didn't Melba's old friends come to her birthday party? In what other ways was her evening a disappointment?** Melba's old friends did not attend her party because they were afraid to come to her house. They felt that she no longer fit in with them, and they wanted to attend another party being held later the same evening. In addition, Melba's conversation with Vince was strained and awkward; she had not found time or energy to return his calls or otherwise maintain their relationship. Furthermore, Melba's mother and grandmother did not allow her to go with Vince to the other party, since it was evening and going out would not be safe for her. Melba felt that the integration had "stolen" her sixteenth birthday.

2. **What was Melba hoping for during Christmas vacation? What happened to spoil her hopes?** Melba was hoping that Christmas vacation would provide a time of rest and relaxation, when she could stop thinking and worrying about the stress and danger she faced at Central High. Unfortunately, two days before the end of school, some boys blocked Minnijean's way in the school cafeteria, kicking her and calling her names. Because Minnijean panicked and spilled hot chili over the heads of two of the boys, she was suspended. Melba and the other African-American students had to spend Christmas vacation attending meetings and worrying about what would happen to Minnijean.

3. **How had the segregationists' attitude changed when school began again in the New Year? What was their goal?** When school began again in the New Year, Melba noticed that the segregationists seemed to have new energy and confidence. Minnijean's suspension gave them new hope that they could make the African-American students leave the school. The segregationists' goal was to provoke the African Americans to misbehave so that they, too, would be suspended or expelled.

4. **Why did Melba begin to doubt she could get through the rest of the year at Central High? Give evidence to show how deeply discouraged she was. How did Grandma India help her at this time?** Melba began to doubt she could get through the school year at Central because the physical and psychological abuse she was subject to was becoming unbearable. She was so discouraged that she wrote in her diary that she wished she were dead, or at least that she could be invisible for a month or two. Grandma India helped Melba see that by giving up, especially by killing herself, she would give satisfaction to the segregationists. Grandma India began spending more time with Melba each day, praying with her and just talking or having fun. She reminded Melba of her family's love for her. She encouraged Melba to take on a project learning about space exploration. She also advised Melba to take her tormentors by surprise by thanking them every time they did something mean to her. This would frustrate their desire to upset her.

5. **Who was Andy? What unexpected help did Melba get when Andy was about to attack her on the street outside the school? How do you think she felt as she drove home?** Andy was a boy who was particularly aggressive toward Melba, calling her vile names, hurting her physically, and threatening to kill her. When Andy was about to attack Melba on the street outside the school, another blonde boy named Link left her the keys to his car so she could drive away safely. Melba felt grateful, but also confused and worried, as she drove home in Link's car, because she did not know why he let her take it or what would happen next

Make a Prediction:

What would happen to Melba as a result of driving away with Link's car?

Guided Discussion:

Discuss some of the key questions and activities in Section II. In addition, feel free to include in your discussion questions that are not in the Discussion Guide. You might want to ask, *What finally happened to Minnijean? Why is this ironic?* Minnijean was expelled from Central after she was attacked with hot soup for a second time on Feb. 6. National leaders of the NAACP arranged for her to have a scholarship to a prestigious high school in New York, living at the home of a world-famous psychologist. It seems ironic that Minnijean, who was expelled from Central High School for her "misbehavior," was then able to attend a prestigious school where she was warmly welcomed, while the other eight students, who managed to remain calm and take the abuse heaped on them, had to go back to Central every day to receive more abuse.

 ## Vocabulary Prediction Check-up

Return to the vocabulary prediction chart, and use it to check the predictions students made prior to reading this section of the book. Remind students that, even if their predictions did not prove true, the value was in making them.

 ## Selection Review

1. **Explain what Danny could and could not do to help Melba. What was his goal? What did he teach Melba about taking care of herself?** Danny followed Melba around the halls. He stepped in if she was in serious danger. He could not argue or fight with students. He could not enter the classrooms, cafeteria, or auditorium. His main goal was to keep her alive. He put out a lit stick of dynamite, and rinsed Melba's eyes when she was attacked with chemicals. He taught her to stay alert and look confident. She learned to ignore minor problems and watch out for serious dangers. She learned to fight back if necessary. She developed the attitude of a soldier in battle.

2. **List some of the ways people tried to lower tensions at Central High School. Explain why these attempts did not succeed.** In one attempt to calm things down, the 101st Airborne Division was taken out of Central High after just a week. The Arkansas National Guardsmen were left in the halls instead. However, the Guardsmen watched the students being abused and did not protect them. A meeting was held between African-American students and segregationist student leaders. It did not work because the segregationists misunderstood the African Americans' position. Another meeting took place between school officials, African-American students, and their parents. It did not succeed because the officials would not accept their responsibility to protect the students.

3. **How were Minnijean Brown's ideas about Central High School different from those of the other eight students? How did her experience at Central High end?** When they realized the dangers they faced at Central High School, the other eight students decided not to call attention to themselves. They just wanted to survive the school year. Minnijean believed that white students would accept her if they could hear her sing. Sadly, the school authorities did not allow her to peform in the Christmas concert. Minnijean became very tense. In December two boys blocked her way and harassed her in the cafeteria. She spilled hot chili over them and was suspended. After another incident occurred in February, Minnijean was expelled from Central High School. The NAACP found a scholarship for her to attend a private high school in New York.

4. **How did integration spoil Melba's plans for her sixteenth birthday and her Christmas vacation?** Melba planned a birthday party with old friends. Except for her boyfriend Vince, the friends did not attend because they were afraid to come to her house. They felt that Melba no longer "fit in" with them. Melba's time with Vince was awkward. He went to another party that night, but she had to stay home because her mother and grandmother were afraid for her to be out late. Minnijean's suspension spoiled Melba's hopes for a restful Christmas vacation. The eight other students spent their time attending meetings and worrying about Minnijean.

5. **After Christmas vacation, the segregationists' attacks became even more violent. How did this affect Melba? How did Grandma India help her conquer her despair?** Melba became very discouraged as the attacks became more violent. She wrote in her diary that she wished she were dead. Grandma India told Melba that if she gave up it would please her attackers. She spent more time with Melba and reminded her of her family's love. She suggested Melba begin a personal project studying space travel. She told Melba to thank her tormentors when they did something mean to her. This would frustrate them.

> **Informational Text Connections**
>
> Types of informational text with connections to this section include:
>
> Biographical information about Mahatma Gandhi
>
> Age-appropriate articles about the use of non-violent resistence in the civil rights movement
>
> A brochure or article geared toward young people about warning signs and prevention of teen suicide (ask your gudance counselor or school psychologist for suggestions)
>
> Select a text appropriate to your students' reading level and interests. Have them read and analyze the text using applicable criteria from the Common Core Standards. (Remember that different texts will lend themselves to different approaches for comprehension and analysis.)

 Literature-Related Writing

1. Write a **list of idioms** you, your friends, your teachers and your family use in the course of a day. (The list should include at least ten idioms, different from the ones listed in the Writer's Craft Box.)

2. Like Melba, many of us have looked forward to a birthday or holiday celebration only to be disappointed when the "big day" finally arrived. Write a **personal narrative** about a disappointing birthday or holiday celebration in your own life. You may choose whether to write a serious or a humorous narrative.

3. Melba wrote an unusual list of New Year's resolutions (page 156). Make a **list** of five or more "resolutions" that you would like to keep in your life – even if New Year's is still a long way off!

Extension Activities

1. Interview someone who experienced school desegregation in the 1950s or 1960s. What challenges did your interviewee face in this situation? What similarities and differences do you notice between this person's experience and that of Melba and her friends? Share what you learn with your classmates.

2. Look in old magazines at the library to learn more about fashions in 1958. Design a wardrobe that Minnijean might have worn as she traveled to the private high school in New York (page 167).

3. Draw a picture illustrating a scene from this section of the book.

Literature Test

1. **Why did the African-American students want the 101st Airborne Division soldiers to guard them rather than the Arkansas National Guardsmen? At the meeting the school officials held with the students and their parents, how was the school officials' attitude similar to that of the National Guardsmen?** The students preferred to have the 101st Airborne Division soldiers guard them because the Arkansas National Guardsmen simply stood around and watched them being abused, making no attempt to intervene. At the meeting with the students and their parents, the school officials refused to address their own responsibility to keep the African-American students safe. Both the Guardsmen and the school officials failed to assume their responsibility to protect the students.

2. **Describe the circumstances that led to Minnijean being suspended, then expelled, from Central High School.** Minnijean became very tense when school officials refused to allow her to participate in the school concert. She spilled chili over the heads of two boys who blocked her way and tormented her in the cafeteria, which led to her suspension. Segregationist students kept harassing her, and after a second incident occurred in February, she was expelled.

3. **Explain how the integration situation "spoiled" Melba's sixteenth birthday, as well as her Christmas vacation.** Most of Melba's old friends did not attend her birthday party because they were afraid to come to her house, and they no longer felt that she "fit in." Even her boyfriend, Vince, was awkward and uncomfortable, and finally left to attend another party. Melba had to stay at home since it was considered dangerous for her

to be out at night. Her Christmas vacation was spoiled by the news of Minnijean's suspension. Melba and the other students spent their time attending meetings and wondering what would happen to Minnijean.

4. **Why did Melba write in her diary that she wished she were dead? List at least two ways that Grandma India helped her change her mind.** Melba wrote that she wished she were dead because the segregationist students' attacks had become more and more violent and frightening. Students should list at least two of the following: Grandma India pointed out to Melba that giving up and killing herself would just satisfy the segregationists. She spent more time with Melba, praying and having fun with her. She reminded her of her family's love for her. She encouraged Melba to begin a personal project studying space travel. She advised Melba that she could frustrate her tormentors by thanking them when they tried to make her miserable.

Discussion Guide #4

Chapters 15-18 and Epilogue (pages 174 - 226)

Vocabulary List A

careened (p. 174)	veneer (p. 187)	*rational (p. 195)
shunned (p. 178)	biannual (p. 187)	lapsed (p. 195)
vocally (p. 179)	garnet (p. 187)	dispassionate (p. 196)
hodgepodge (p. 179)	rummaged (p. 188)	dismal (p. 197)
averted (p. 179)	remnants (p. 188)	feeble (p. 199)
*bizarre (p. 181)	caressing (p. 189)	taut (p. 199)
heeded (p. 185)	forbade (p. 190)	protruding (p. 199)
*vital (p. 185)	acclaimed (p. 191)	*immaculate (p. 199)
justified (v., p. 186)	temporarily (p. 191)	staples (n., p. 199)
catastrophe (p. 186)	*complexity (p. 192)	emaciated (p. 200)
heirlooms (p. 187)	violate (p. 193)	provision (p. 201)
mementos (p. 187)	reminiscing (p. 194)	harping (p. 202)
glossy (p. 187)	vicarious (p. 195)	

Special Glossary of Idiomatic Expressions

twixt the devil and the deep blue sea - forced to choose between two unpleasant options

cloak-and-dagger - secret; mysterious; undercover

filled to the rafters - very full

work herself up into a lather - become very disturbed and agitated

---

Glossary of Starred Words

bizarre - strange; unusual

vital - very important

complexity - the quality of being complicated

rational - reasonable; logical

immaculate - spotlessly clean

TEACHER'S MANUAL
Chapters 15-18 and Epilogue

Sample Meaningful Sentences for Starred Words

1. We had never seen anything like Mr. Twembley's **bizarre** outfit: pointed red boots, a furry blue hat and pajama pants.

2. The lawyer told the judge that he had just received **vital** information that could completely change the outcome of the trial.

3. Mr. Hornsby tries to give our chemistry class clear, simple explanations, but the **complexity** of the subject itself makes it hard for us to understand.

4. Father was a very **rational** man who liked to base all important decisions on logical reasoning.

5. Mama decorated the tables for the reception with **immaculate** snowy white napkins, freshly laundered and pressed, folded beside each dinner plate.

The Writer's Craft

Suspense

Suspense is the condition of fear or uncertainty that makes us want to keep reading so we can find out "what happens next." Sometimes writers create suspense by describing a strange or frightening setting, like a haunted house or a stormy night. Sometimes suspense is created through the use of mysterious characters - a shadowy figure in a black cape, perhaps, or a silent man with his hat pulled down over his eyes. But in many cases, suspense is created simply by describing puzzling or alarming situations.

You've probably noticed when you watch television that the commercials often come just when the main characters are in the most suspenseful situations. Of course! The director wants you to keep watching so you can find out what happens next. Similarly, writers often end a chapter with a suspenseful situation to make you want to keep reading. For example, chapter 14 ended with Melba driving home in Link's car, wondering why he let her take it and what would happen to her. As you read chapters 15-17, watch for other mysterious or alarming situations that make you want to keep reading.

Talent Development Secondary Program

DISCUSSION QUESTIONS AND ACTIVITIES

Section I. Read chapters 15-17 (pages 174-203). Discuss answers to the following questions with a classmate, then write your answers separately.

1. **Why did Grandma India hurry to cover Link's car with old sheets when Melba drove home in it? Explain Grandma's and Mother's concerns about this situation. How were their worries put to rest?** Grandma India hurried to cover the car with sheets because she did not want anyone, especially the police, to see the car parked in their yard. At first, Grandma and Mother were afraid that perhaps Link would call the police and accuse Melba of stealing his car. After a little while had passed, they began to worry about how they would return the car to Link without anyone finding out what had happened. Link solved this problem by suggesting that Melba leave the car in front of a popular ice cream parlor.

2. **What happened between Melba and the white boys who harassed her in the cafeteria? Why did she feel good about the way she handled this situation? Why did she feel angry and distrustful toward Link?** One day when Melba had to sit alone in the cafeteria, a group of white boys sat nearby. They began threatening and insulting her. Soon they started throwing things at her. When the bell rang, the boys stayed in their seats, and Melba knew if she tried to leave the cafeteria they would start a fight and she would be blamed. She waited patiently, reading her book. Finally, when the second bell rang, the boys left. Melba was surprised to see that Link was part of the group. He even seemed to be a ringleader. Melba was confused and furious, and felt that he could not truly be her friend if he behaved this way toward her when he was with other white boys.

3. **How did Link explain his behavior in the cafeteria? Describe the friendship that developed between Melba and Link.** Link told Melba that he had joined the group in the cafeteria because his father made him attend the segregationist's planning meetings, and he knew that they intended to involve her in a confrontation. He hoped that by joining the group he could prevent them from seriously harming her. He pointed out that he had "saved her skin" by persuading the boys to leave the cafeteria when the second bell rang. Melba and Link developed a secret friendship. Link did not want anyone at school to

TEACHER'S MANUAL
Chapters 15-18 and Epilogue

know that he was secretly warning her about the segregationists' plans, so they spoke only on the telephone.

4. **Why were Melba's mother and grandmother concerned about this friendship? Why did Melba continue her friendship with Link in spite of her mother and grandmother's distrust?** Melba's mother and grandmother were afraid that Link might be "setting Melba up," pretending to be nice so that he could lure her into a trap. Melba continued to talk with Link, although she too wondered exactly what Link's motives were, because she realized that Link could provide her with vital, "inside" information that would help her to avoid danger at Central.

5. **Describe the North Little Rock community. Why did Link ask Melba to meet him there? Why did Melba decide she could trust Link after she met Nana Healey and heard her story?** North Little Rock was a very poor African-American community. Many of its people lived in run-down "chicken-shack" houses, and ragged men clustered on the corners drinking liquor. Link asked Melba to meet him there because he wanted to introduce her to Nana Healey, who had been his nanny. She lived alone and was seriously ill. Link hoped that Melba could persuade Nana Healey to see a doctor. When she met Nana Healey and heard her story, Melba realized that Link had cared for her for a long time, coming to see her and providing her with food since his parents had failed to do so. Melba understood then that Link's friendship was sincere.

6. **What change did Melba notice in her mother's behavior? How did the school board put pressure on Mother Lois to withdraw Melba from Central High School?** Melba noticed that her mother was becoming tense and quiet. The school board put pressure on her by informing her that her teaching contract would not be renewed unless she withdrew Melba from Central High School immediately.

Make A Prediction:

What do you think would have happened if Melba had refused to trust Link?

Talent Development Secondary Program

Guided Discussion:

Discuss some of the key questions in Section I. In addition, feel free to include in your discussion questions that are not in the Discussion Guide. Make sure to discuss the question raised in the Writer's Craft Box on "Suspense." The author leaves readers in suspense at the end of each chapter. For example, at the end of chapter 15 the reader is left wondering what Link's real motives are, and whether he is really a racist, as his comments would seem to indicate. Chapter 16 ends with the appointment of Judge Lemley to hear the Little Rock School Board's petition for a postponement of integration, and Melba's concerns about the implications of this hearing. Chapter 17 ends with the termination of Mother Lois' teaching contract. The reader wonders whether she will indeed lose her job, and if she does, how her family will survive.

Take time to discuss with your students Melba's decision to go against her mother's wishes in her friendship with Link, and even to lie to her mother and grandmother when she went to meet Link in North Little Rock. Ask students what they would have done in Melba's place, and why. Point out to them that Melba's decision was not made lightly, but only after careful thought and discussion with her mother and grandmother. While they did not agree with Melba, her mother and grandmother tacitly allowed her to continue this friendship, perhaps realizing that she had valid reasons to do so. Melba actually lied to her mother only once, when she sensed a real urgency and desperation in Link's voice, and she did later draw her grandmother into her attempts to help Link care for Nana Healey. Help students to realize that while there can be valid reasons to follow a course of action contrary to one's parents' wishes, this decision should be taken only in extreme cases, after careful consideration and discussion with the parents.

Ask students, *How did Link explain his decision to secretly help Melba instead of going along with his family and friends?* Link explained his commitment to helping Melba by saying that he wanted to enjoy the activities of his senior year. If he could prevent something terrible from happening, perhaps the graduation and pre-graduation activities could be held as usual, and people around the country would stop considering Central High School a "bad" place.

TEACHER'S MANUAL
Chapters 15-18 and Epilogue

 Vocabulary Prediction Check-up

Return to the vocabulary prediction chart, and use it to check the predictions students made prior to reading this section of the reading selection. Remind students that, even if their predictions did not prove true, the value was in making them.

Vocabulary List B

reinstate (p. 204)
caliber (p. 205)
drastic (p. 206)
inclusion (p. 206)
tainted (v., p. 207)
snippets (p. 207)
*speculate (p. 207)
ordeal (p. 207)
warranted (p. 209)
grueling (adj., p. 209)
*accolades (p. 210)
forthcoming (p. 210)
impostor (p. 212)
baccalaureate (p. 214)
whim (p. 214)
conferred (p. 217)
luxurious (p. 217)
hobnobbed (p. 217)
exerted (p. 218)
entanglement (p. 219)
ultimately (p. 219)
bounty (p. 219)
unconditional (p. 219)
*tenacious (p. 220)
enclave (p. 220)
suite (p. 220)
*prestigious (p. 221)
livid (p. 221)
ferry (v., p. 221)
interdependence (p. 222)
ravages (n., p. 222)
tedious (p. 223)
alumni (p. 223)
dignitaries (p. 223)
lavish (v., p. 223)
ascend (p. 224)
camaraderie (p. 224)
thriving (p. 225)
*impeccably (p. 226)

Special Glossary

teletyped - sent out a typed message over the telegraph system

leukemia - a form of cancer that affects the blood system

Quakers - members of the Society of Friends, a Christian religious tradition strongly committed to pacifism and social justice

> ### Glossary of Starred Words
> **speculate** - to guess
>
> **accolades** - high praises
>
> **tenacious** - determined; stubborn; persistent
>
> **prestigious** - esteemed; highly respected
>
> **impeccably** - perfectly; spotlessly; immaculately

Talent Development Secondary Program

Sample Meaningful Sentences for Starred Words

1. Since no one told us why our teacher was absent, we began to **speculate**, making both reasonable and crazy guesses about where she might be.

2. Mr. Hanson covered Raymond with **accolades** at the assembly, praising him in almost every area as he awarded him the Faculty Prize for Academic and Personal Excellence.

3. The watchdog had such a **tenacious** grip on the burglar's leg that he did not let go even when the man hit him on the head.

4. Jerome attended a college that was so **prestigious** that several companies offered him jobs just because of the school's excellent reputation.

5. Little Danny was **impeccably** dressed in a white linen suit for his sister's wedding, so his mom told him to be extra careful not to get dirty.

The Writer's Craft

Epilogue

The **epilogue** is literally an "afterword." Books often include an epilogue to tell us about what happened later, after the period in which the story is set. Most of *Warriors Don't Cry* tells us about the writer's experiences in 1957-58, the school year during which she participated in the difficult task of integrating Central High School. Chapter 18 goes on to briefly summarize her experiences in the years immediately following. The epilogue, however, describes a very special moment: the thirty-year reunion at which the nine African-American alumni returned to Little Rock and to Central High School so that the world could honor their achievement and celebrate the progress made since that time. As you read the epilogue, watch for reasons the author gives for feeling both pain and joy on that historic occasion.

DISCUSSION QUESTIONS AND ACTIVITIES

Section II. Read chapter 18 and the Epilogue (pp. 204-226). Discuss your responses to the questions and activities with a classmate. Then write your answers separately.

1. **List the steps that Melba's mother took to pressure the school board to renew her teaching contract. How did she finally succeed?** After several personal visits to school headquarters to plead her case, Melba's mother contacted reporters from several white newspapers and furnished them the details of her case. One newspaper published the article, and national wire services carried it to newspapers in other cities. Soon telephone calls began pouring in from all over the country protesting the school board's actions. However, the authorities still did not renew the contract. Finally, Mother asked for help from African-American church leaders. One of the most prominent of them, Bishop Sherman, advised her to tell the white administrator, "Bishop Sherman asked me to tell you he would like me to have a job." The day after she did this, Mother's supervisor came to see her in her classroom and told her that she was an excellent teacher and that she would have her job back the following year.

2. **How did Melba mark the end of her school year at Central High School? Why were she and the other African-American students not allowed to attend the graduation ceremony?** The end of Melba's school year at Central was a day like any other day. However, her mother gave her a new outfit to commemorate the occasion, and Grandma India advised her to burn her school papers, as well as a list of all the people at Central High who had wronged her, to symbolize letting go of the pain and anger she still felt about the experience. Melba and the other African-American students were not allowed to attend the graduation ceremonies because the authorities felt that their presence would make it even more difficult to control the crowd and protect the family and guests of Ernest Green, who was graduating.

3. **Why did Link insist that Melba meet with him the day after graduation? What did he want her to do? Explain why Melba responded the way she did.** Link insisted that Melba meet him the day after graduation because Nana Healey had just passed away, and he was very upset. He wanted Melba to come with him when he went north to attend college. Melba finally agreed to think about this proposition in order to get Link to calm down. However, she knew that she would not go with him. Melba

probably realized that in his grief over Nana Healey's death, Link was not thinking clearly about the implications of his suggestion. Melba was only sixteen and had not completed high school, so it would be very foolish for her to run away from home. She knew that an interracial romantic relationship (especially in the 1950's) would involve serious social and emotional tensions that she was not ready to take on at that time. Also, Melba and Link had known each other as friends, but not at a romantic level. Their relationship up to this point had certainly not prepared them for marriage or for living together.

4. **Describe Melba's life during the 1958-59 school year. How and where did she finally finish high school?** During the 1958-59 school year, Melba stayed home. Faced with a court order to continue with integration, Governor Faubus simply closed all of Little Rock's high schools. Melba felt lonely and isolated, because in addition to rejection and hatred from white segregationists, she face resentment from the African-American community since people lost their jobs and businesses as they were pressured to talk the students out of returning to Central High. On October 24, Melba's beloved Grandma India passed away, so Melba spent most of the year waiting at home alone. In September 1959, the NAACP arranged for her to go to California. She lived with George and Carol McCabe and their four children, a warmhearted white family who welcomed her as if she were their own daughter. George McCabe was a professor at San Francisco State University, and after Melba completed high school he helped her enroll at SFSU.

5. **Describe Melba's emotions at the thirty-year reunion of the "Little Rock Nine." Remember that *irony* is a word used to describe a situation that turns out very differently from what was expected. What was *ironic* about the circumstances of the nine alumni's return visit to Central High School?** Melba's emotions at the thirty-year reunion ranged from joy at meeting friends she had not seen in many years, to rediscovery of a part of herself she had lost touch with, to pain at the ever-present memories of the torture that had been inflicted on her and her comrades at Central High School. It is ironic that when they returned to Central High School, a school where so much time, energy, and money had been spent to exclude African-American students, the student body president who came to greet them in 1987 was himself an African-American student.

TEACHER'S MANUAL
Chapters 15-18 and Epilogue

What If.

What do you think might have happened if Melba had agreed to run away from home, as Link suggested?

Guided Discussion:

Discuss some of the key questions in Section II. In addition, feel free to include in your discussion questions that are not in the Discussion Guide. Be sure to emphasize the wisdom of Melba's decision *not* to run away from home to live near Link when he went to college.

Melba says that integrating Central High School cost the nine African-American students "much, much more" than half a million dollars: "It cost us our innocence and a precious year of our teenage lives" (page 216). Ask students to list some of the things that the students sacrificed in their commitment to integration. Answers might include their friendships with students at their former schools, normal social life, the chance to participate in sports, music, and other extra-curricular activities, freedom of movement (especially at night), peace of mind, physical health and well-being.

 Vocabulary Prediction Check-up

Return to the vocabulary prediction chart, and use it to check the predictions students made prior to reading this section of the book. Remind students that, even if their predictions did not prove true, the value was in making them.

Selection Review

1. **How did Link try to help Melba? Why did she feel suspicious toward him? Why did she decide to trust him in spite of her fears?** Link tried to help Melba secretly, without letting his friends know. He attended segregationists' meetings and learned their plans. Then he telephoned Melba to tell her how to avoid dangerous situations. Once Link joined a group of boys who were tormenting Melba. He pretended to go along with them but suggested they wait until later to "get" her. Melba was suspicious of Link for several reasons. Her mother and grandmother warned that Link might make her trust him, then draw her into a trap. Also, when he was with the troublemakers she heard him use racist words just as they did. Melba finally decided to trust Link because he provided her with useful information. No one else could help her in this way.

2. **Link's family and friends were all segregationists. What reasons did he give for to trying to help Melba? When Melba went with him to visit Nana Healey, what did she understand about his real motives?** Link said that he was trying to help Melba so that nothing terrible would happen to spoil his senior year. He wanted people to stop thinking that Central High was such a terrible place. However, when Melba went with Link to visit Nana Healey, she saw how much he cared for her. Nana Healey had worked for Link's parents for many years. Link was angry and bitter that they had failed to provide for her. Melba saw that Link was upset about white people treating African-Americans unfairly. She understood that his friendship toward her was also sincere.

3. **Why did the Little Rock school board take Mother's teaching job away? How did she finally persuade them to renew the contract?** The school board refused to renew Mother's contract unless she took Melba out of Central High School. Mother begged them to change their minds. This did not work, so she persuaded a white newspaper to publish the story. Calls and letters poured in criticizing the school board's action. However, the problem was not solved. It was solved only after an African-American church leader gave Mother a message for the school administrator. The message was that Bishop Sherman wanted Mother to have her job back. The contract was renewed.

4. **Why was Melba disappointed at the graduation arrangements? Why did Link insist on meeting with her the next day?** Melba was disappointed that she and the other African-American students were not allowed to attend graduation. The authorities said that they had to focus on protecting Ernie and his family. Link insisted on seeing Melba because he was very upset. Nana Healey had passed away on graduation day. Link tried to persuade Melba to come with him when he went north to attend college. Melba agreed to "think about it," but she knew that she would not go with him.

5. **Why did Melba finally go to California to finish high school? Describe some of the emotions she experienced when she returned to Central High School thirty years later.** In order to stop the integration, Governor Faubus closed all Little Rock high schools for a full year. The following year, the NAACP arranged for Melba to live with a family in California so she could finish high school. When Melba returned to Central for the thirty-year reunion, she was thrilled to meet her friends. She had not seen some of them in many years. She felt she was rediscovering a part of herself she had lost. However, she also felt the pain of her fear and suffering at Central. She was pleased to notice that the president of the student body was an African American.

Informational Text Connections

Types of informational text with connections to this section include:

- News articles about changes in personnel or policy in your local school district (for controversial topics, try to find articles representing more than one viewpoint)
- Biographical information about Melba Patillo Beals' adult life and career
- Biographical information about Ernest Green and other members of the "Little Rock Nine"

Select a text appropriate to your students' reading level and interests. Have them read and analyze the text using applicable criteria from the Common Core Standards. (Remember that different texts will lend themselves to different approaches for comprehension and analysis.)

Literature-Related Writing

1. Pretend you are a newspaper reporter in 1958. Write a **news article** about Mother losing her teaching job because of Melba's attending Central High School.

2. Letters poured in from all over the country protesting the school board's decision. Choose a controversial topic you feel strongly about. Write a **persuasive letter** explaining your position. Send a copy of the letter to a newspaper, to an elected official, or to an administrator with appropriate decision-making authority.

3. Melba says that the McCabes "became the loving, nurturing bridge over which I walked to adulthood" (page 219). Later she describes Link as "a hero… sent to ferry me over a rough spot in my life's path" (page 221). Think of someone who has been a "bridge" or a "ferry" to help you get through an important or difficult time in your life. In a **personal reflection**, describe this person (or these people). Tell how he, she, or they helped you.

 Extension Activities

1. Draw or paint a portrait of Nana Healey in her home, based on the description given in chapter 17.

2. Using the Internet or library resources, obtain a transcript or listen to a tape of the interview with Melba Patillo Beals conducted by Brian Lamb on the program "Booknotes," which aired November 27, 1994. Share what you learn with your classmates.

Literature Test

1. **Explain how Link helped Melba. List three reasons why Link helped her this way.** Link helped Melba by providing her with "inside information" about the segregationist's plans to harass and abuse her. Students should list any three of the following reasons: Link wanted to make sure that nothing terrible happened to spoil his senior year. He wanted people to stop thinking that Central High was such a terrible place. His affection for Nana Healey and his anger at the way his parents had treated her made him sensitive to racial injustice. He also genuinely cared about Melba and her well-being.

2. **How did the school board try to force Melba's mother to take her out of Central High School? How was this problem solved?** The school board took Mother's teaching job away in an attempt to force her to withdraw Melba from Central High. This problem was finally solved when Mother went to the administrator with a message from one of the African-American bishops, stating that he wanted Mother to have her job.

3. **Why did Melba agree to see Link the day after graduation? Tell what happened at their meeting.** Melba agreed to see Link the day after graduation because she knew he was upset about Nana Healey's death. Link became very excited and insisted that Melba come with him to the North when he went to college. Melba agreed to think about it just to calm him down, but she knew she would never see him again.

4. **Explain why Melba was both glad and sad when she went back to Central High School for the thirty-year reunion.** Melba was glad to see old friends and rediscover a part of herself that she had lost. She was also glad to see that the president of the student body at Central was a young African-American. However, she was sad because she remembered all the pain and fear she had experienced at Central High School.

Selection Review #1

Warriors Don't Cry

Introduction and Chapters 1 - 4

1. **How did the writer make sure that the account found in *Warriors Don't Cry* would be accurate, even though she wrote it many years later?** The writer based her account on many sources written at the time the events were occurring. For example, she used her own personal diary and the notes that her mother took at that time. Her mother had also collected a number of newspaper articles about the school's integration. Because she relied on these sources, the writer is confident that her story is an accurate one.

2. **List some of the problems Melba faced as a child because of racism. What were two situations in which she narrowly escaped tragedy?** As a child, Melba learned that African Americans had to use the worst fountains and rest rooms. She could not ride the merry-go-round at the park. Her parents were forced to back down, embarrassed, when a white grocer overcharged them. As a baby, Melba almost died because a white nurse did not want to give her the proper care that the doctor had ordered. Later, when she was twelve, she was almost raped by a white man who was angry about the Supreme Court decision on the integration of schools.

3. **What did Melba find amazing about Cincinnati, Ohio? Why did she have to return to Little Rock, and how did her life change at that point?** Melba found Cincinnati amazing because there was no segregation. She and her mother could go shopping downtown without stepping aside to let white people pass. They were invited to dinner at the home of her uncle's white neighbor. They could go to a movie with white people or eat dinner in a restaurant served by white waiters. Melba wanted to stay in Cincinnati to finish high school. However, she had to return to Little Rock because she had been chosen to attend Central High School, an all-white school. When Melba arrived in Little Rock, her life and her family's life were taken up with meetings and preparation for the integration.

4. **Melba decided to participate in the integration even though she was afraid for herself and her family. Why? What qualities did she have in common with the other eight students taking part?** Melba was afraid for herself and her family because they received many threatening phone calls. She decided to participate in the integration anyway because she believed this could be the first step toward ending segregation in Little Rock. She hoped the white students would change their attitudes when they got to know African Americans as classmates. Like the other eight students chosen for the integration, Melba was a serious student. She attended church regularly and was respectful and well mannered. Like the others, she was an independent-minded, proud person who planned to attend college.

continued...

Talent Development Secondary Program

5. **Describe Melba's frightening experience the first day she was supposed to attend Central High. How did her grandmother deal with Melba's fears and thoughts of quitting?** The first day Melba was to attend Central High School, she and her mother could not get near the school because of the crowd. They watched soldiers and crowd members bullying Melba's friend Elizabeth. Then they realized that they were also in danger. They just reached their car in time to escape a mob of angry white men. In spite of this, Melba's grandmother would not let her quit and go back to the black high school. She said that if Melba gave up, the segregationists would believe they were free to treat African Americans unfairly. Grandma told Melba that she was a soldier on God's battlefield. She said that Melba must learn not to cry despite her pain and fear.

Selection Review #2

Warriors Don't Cry

Chapters 5 - 8

1. **Describe some ways that African Americans, and a few white people, showed support for Melba and the other eight students.** Community members showed support in many ways. African-American churches encouraged the students and prayed for them. NAACP leaders and lawyers advised them about the legal hearings. Teachers of both races lent them books and tutored them so they would not fall behind in their schoolwork. A white man paid for an ad in the paper. This ad said all citizens of Arkansas should be ashamed of the hatred and bigotry that had been shown to the students.

2. **In what ways did the journalists' behavior encourage and inspire Melba?** Melba was surprised that the white journalists called her "Miss" and treated her respectfully. She saw that black and white reporters treated each other as friends. She saw that the integration would not be taking place if the reporters had not been so brave and determined to tell the world what was happening. Melba felt even more convinced that integration was right. She thought she might like to be a journalist herself one day.

3. **List some reasons for Melba's feelings of surprise at the federal court hearing. What was decided in the hearing?** Melba was surprised that the courtroom was so small. Also, up close the national guardsmen seemed so ordinary. Melba was very surprised that Governor Faubus did not attend the hearing. Even the governor's lawyers walked out almost as soon as the hearing began. Judge Davies decided that the integration would continue. He said that Governor Faubus had no right to stop it.

4. **What did the Central High School building make Melba think of? Why? Why was this *ironic*?** Central High School reminded Melba of a museum or a beautiful castle. It was very big and had beautiful stone walls, marble floors, and spiral staircases. This was ironic because Melba soon discovered that Central High School would instead be a place of danger and fear for her.

5. **List some of the good and bad things that happened to Melba on her first day at Central High School. How did she describe her day in her article for the Associated Press?** Melba's first day at Central High School was like a nightmare. People called her names. A woman spit in her face. Students tormented her in class. A group of women even came over the fence to attack her on the playing field. She lost her way. Worst of all, she heard policemen saying they might let the crowd hang one of the students in order to save the others. However, a few people showed kindness to the students. Mrs. Huckaby, the girls' vice principal, tried to treat them

continued...

Talent Development Secondary Program

fairly. Melba's gym teacher and her shorthand teacher, Mrs. Pickwick, showed concern for her. The Assistant Police Chief and the police drivers risked their lives to make sure all the students arrived home safely. In her article, however, Melba told only part of the truth. She was afraid that if she told how terrible it really was, the integration would be stopped.

6. **Explain why President Eisenhower sent the Airborne Division soldiers to Central High School. What difference did the soldiers make on Melba's second day of school?** The soldiers were sent to Central High School to protect the nine students and keep the peace. They guarded the students and took them to school. Then a soldier walked through the halls with each student during the day. Melba felt safer on her second day because of the soldiers, especially her "bodyguard," Danny. Still, there were many places where Danny was not allowed to go with her. These places included the classrooms, cafeteria, study hall, and of course the girls' rest rooms and locker room.

Talent Development Secondary Program

Selection Review #3

Warriors Don't Cry

Chapters 9 - 14

1. **Explain what Danny could and could not do to help Melba. What was his goal? What did he teach Melba about taking care of herself?** Danny followed Melba around the halls. He stepped in if she was in serious danger. He could not argue or fight with students. He could not enter the classrooms, cafeteria, or auditorium. His main goal was to keep her alive. He put out a lit stick of dynamite, and rinsed Melba's eyes when she was attacked with chemicals. He taught her to stay alert and look confident. She learned to ignore minor problems and watch out for serious dangers. She learned to fight back if necessary. She developed the attitude of a soldier in battle.

2. **List some of the ways people tried to lower tensions at Central High School. Explain why these attempts did not succeed.** In one attempt to calm things down, the 101st Airborne Division was taken out of Central High after just a week. The Arkansas National Guardsmen were left in the halls instead. However, the Guardsmen watched the students being abused and did not protect them. A meeting was held between African-American students and segregationist student leaders. It did not work because the segregationists misunderstood the African Americans' position. Another meeting took place between school officials, African-American students, and their parents. It did not succeed because the officials would not accept their responsibility to protect the students.

3. **How were Minnijean Brown's ideas about Central High School different from those of the other eight students? How did her experience at Central High end?** When they realized the dangers they faced at Central High School, the other eight students decided not to call attention to themselves. They just wanted to survive the school year. Minnijean believed that white students would accept her if they could hear her sing. Sadly, the school authorities did not allow her to peform in the Christmas concert. Minnijean became very tense. In December two boys blocked her way and harassed her in the cafeteria. She spilled hot chili over them and was suspended. After another incident occurred in February, Minnijean was expelled from Central High School. The NAACP found a scholarship for her to attend a private high school in New York.

4. **How did integration spoil Melba's plans for her sixteenth birthday and her Christmas vacation?** Melba planned a birthday party with old friends. Except for her boyfriend Vince, the friends did not attend because they were afraid to come to her house. They felt that Melba no longer "fit in" with them. Melba's time with Vince was awkward. He went to another party that night,

continued...

but she had to stay home because her mother and grandmother were afraid for her to be out late. Minnijean's suspension spoiled Melba's hopes for a restful Christmas vacation. The eight other students spent their time attending meetings and worrying about Minnijean.

5. **After Christmas vacation, the segregationists' attacks became even more violent. How did this affect Melba? How did Grandma India help her conquer her despair?** Melba became very discouraged as the attacks became more violent. She wrote in her diary that she wished she were dead. Grandma India told Melba that if she gave up it would please her attackers. She spent more time with Melba and reminded her of her family's love. She suggested Melba begin a personal project studying space travel. She told Melba to thank her tormentors when they did something mean to her. This would frustrate them.

Selection Review #4

Warriors Don't Cry

Chapter 15 - 18 and Epilogue

1. **How did Link try to help Melba? Why did she feel suspicious toward him? Why did she decide to trust him in spite of her fears?** Link tried to help Melba secretly, without letting his friends know. He attended segregationists' meetings and learned their plans. Then he telephoned Melba to tell her how to avoid dangerous situations. Once Link joined a group of boys who were tormenting Melba. He pretended to go along with them but suggested they wait until later to "get" her. Melba was suspicious of Link for several reasons. Her mother and grandmother warned that Link might make her trust him, then draw her into a trap. Also, when he was with the troublemakers she heard him use racist words just as they did. Melba finally decided to trust Link because he provided her with useful information. No one else could help her in this way.

2. **Link's family and friends were all segregationists. What reasons did he give for to trying to help Melba? When Melba went with him to visit Nana Healey, what did she understand about his real motives?** Link said that he was trying to help Melba so that nothing terrible would happen to spoil his senior year. He wanted people to stop thinking that Central High was such a terrible place. However, when Melba went with Link to visit Nana Healey, she saw how much he cared for her. Nana Healey had worked for Link's parents for many years. Link was angry and bitter that they had failed to provide for her. Melba saw that Link was upset about white people treating African-Americans unfairly. She understood that his friendship toward her was also sincere.

3. **Why did the Little Rock school board take Mother's teaching job away? How did she finally persuade them to renew the contract?** The school board refused to renew Mother's contract unless she took Melba out of Central High School. Mother begged them to change their minds. This did not work, so she persuaded a white newspaper to publish the story. Calls and letters poured in criticizing the school board's action. However, the problem was not solved. It was solved only after an African-American church leader gave Mother a message for the school administrator. The message was that Bishop Sherman wanted Mother to have her job back. The contract was renewed.

continued...

4. **Why was Melba disappointed at the graduation arrangements? Why did Link insist on meeting with her the next day?** Melba was disappointed that she and the other African-American students were not allowed to attend graduation. The authorities said that they had to focus on protecting Ernie and his family. Link insisted on seeing Melba because he was very upset. Nana Healey had passed away on graduation day. Link tried to persuade Melba to come with him when he went north to attend college. Melba agreed to "think about it," but she knew that she would not go with him.

5. **Why did Melba finally go to California to finish high school? Describe some of the emotions she experienced when she returned to Central High School thirty years later.** In order to stop the integration, Governor Faubus closed all Little Rock high schools for a full year. The following year, the NAACP arranged for Melba to live with a family in California so she could finish high school. When Melba returned to Central for the thirty-year reunion, she was thrilled to meet her friends. She had not seen some of them in many years. She felt she was rediscovering a part of herself she had lost. However, she also felt the pain of her fear and suffering at Central. She was pleased to notice that the president of the student body was an African American.

Literature Test #1

Warriors Don't Cry

Introduction and Chapters 1 - 4

1. Describe the sources the writer used to make sure the story told in *Warriors Don't Cry* would be accurate.

2. Describe two painful experiences Melba had as a child because of racism.

continued...

Talent Development Secondary Program

3. What did Melba hope to accomplish by participating in the integration of Central High School? Why was this a difficult and courageous decision on her part?

4. After Melba's frightening first attempt to go to Central High School, she felt like giving up on integration. How did her grandmother respond to Melba's fear and discouragement? Why?

Literature Test #2

Warriors Don't Cry

Chapters 5 - 8

1. List three things that encouraged Melba as she waited for the court hearing to allow her to go back to Central High School.

2. Describe the outcome of the federal court hearing. Tell why it was important.

continued...

Talent Development Secondary Program

3. How had Melba imagined Central High School in her dreams? What was it really like for her?

4. Why did the 101st Airborne Division come to Little Rock? How did Melba's experience at school change after the soldiers arrived?

Literature Test #3

Warriors Don't Cry

Chapters 9 - 14

1. Why did the African-American students want the 101st Airborne Division soldiers to guard them rather than the Arkansas National Guardsmen? At the meeting the school officials held with the students and their parents, how was the school officials' attitude similar to that of the National Guardsmen?

2. Describe the circumstances that led to Minnijean being suspended, then expelled, from Central High School.

continued...

3. Explain how the integration situation "spoiled" Melba's sixteenth birthday, as well as her Christmas vacation.

4. Why did Melba write in her diary that she wished she were dead? List at least two ways that Grandma India helped her change her mind.

Name: _____

Literature Test #4

Warriors Don't Cry

Chapters 15 - 18 and Epilogue

1. Explain how Link helped Melba. List three reasons why Link helped her this way.

   _____
   _____
   _____
   _____
   _____
   _____
   _____
   _____
   _____

2. How did the school board try to force Melba's mother to take her out of Central High School? How was this problem solved?

   _____
   _____
   _____
   _____
   _____
   _____
   _____
   _____
   _____

continued...

Talent Development Secondary Program

3. Why did Melba agree to see Link the day after graduation? Tell what happened at their meeting.

_____
_____
_____
_____
_____
_____
_____
_____

4. Explain why Melba was both glad and sad when she went back to Central High School for the thirty-year reunion.

_____
_____
_____
_____
_____
_____
_____
_____

Name: _____

Vocabulary Test #1

Warriors Don't Cry

Introduction and Chapters 1 - 4

WRITE MEANINGFUL SENTENCES FOR THE FOLLOWING WORDS:

cherished	significant	federal
apprehension	hazardous	futile
vulnerable	emphatic	anticipation
	individualists	

_____
_____
_____
_____
_____
_____
_____
_____
_____
_____
_____
_____
_____

Talent Development Secondary Program

Name: _____

Vocabulary Test #2

Warriors Don't Cry

Chapters 5 - 8

WRITE MEANINGFUL SENTENCES FOR THE FOLLOWING WORDS:

aggression	precedent	contempt
initiated	preliminary	jeopardize
dilemma	treacherous	confronted
	compassion	

_____
_____
_____
_____
_____
_____
_____
_____
_____
_____
_____
_____
_____
_____

Talent Development Secondary Program

Name: _____

Vocabulary Test #3

Warriors Don't Cry

Chapters 9 - 14

WRITE MEANINGFUL SENTENCES FOR THE FOLLOWING WORDS:

deteriorated	exclude	incite
mobile	adamant	turmoil
obsessed	console	contends
	intervening	

Name: _____

Vocabulary Test #4

Warriors Don't Cry

Chapters 15 - 18 and Epilogue

WRITE MEANINGFUL SENTENCES FOR THE FOLLOWING WORDS:

bizarre	rational	tenacious
vital	immaculate	prestigious
complexity	speculate	impeccably
	accolades	

Student Team Literature Discussion Guides are available for the following titles:

Non-fiction

- The Acorn People
- Anne Frank: The Diary of a Young Girl
- Barack Obama: President for a New Era
- Barack Obama: United States President
- The Double Life of Pocahontas
- First They Killed My Father
- Freedom Train
- Freedom's Children
- Leon's Story
- One More River to Cross: the Stories of Twelve Black Americans
- Warriors Don't Cry
- We Beat the Street
- What's the Big Idea, Ben Franklin?

Short Stories, Poetry, and Mythology

- Beowulf: A New Telling
- The Dark-Thirty: Southern Tales of the Supernatural
- A Dime a Dozen
- The Dream Keeper and Other Poems
- ego-tripping and other poems for young people
- Keeping the Night Watch
- The Library Card
- Locomotion
- Make Lemonade
- The Odyssey, retold by Robin Lister

Novels

- The Big Wave
- Bridge to Terabithia
- Bud, Not Buddy
- The Bully
- Call It Courage
- The Call of the Wild
- The Cay
- Crash
- Curse of a Winter Moon
- Darnell Rock Reporting
- A Day No Pigs Would Die
- Eddie's Ordeal
- Esperanza Rising
- Fast Sam, Cool Clyde, and Stuff
- Freak the Mighty
- The Giver
- Hatchet
- The Hobbit
- Holes
- In the Night, on Lanvale Street
- Jacob Have I Loved
- Johnny Tremain
- Journey
- Justin and the Best Biscuits in the World
- M. C. Higgins the Great
- Maniac Magee
- The Midwife's Apprentice
- Monster
- The Mystery of Apartment A-13
- Ninjas, Piranhas, and Galileo
- Nothing But the Truth
- Number the Stars
- The Outsiders
- The Pinballs
- Roll of Thunder, Hear My Cry
- Sing Down the Moon
- The Skin I'm In
- To Kill a Mockingbird
- Touching Spirit Bear
- Tuck Everlasting
- The Watsons Go to Birmingham—1963
- The Westing Game
- The Whipping Boy
- Wringer
- A Wrinkle in Time
- Yolonda's Genius

For a catalog and ordering information, call 410-516-4339
For information on Student Team Literature professional development,
call Maria Waltemeyer (410-516-2247)
or visit the Talent Development Secondary website at
www.talentdevelopmentsecondary.com

Made in the USA
Monee, IL
14 August 2024